VOCABULARIO

DEL

IDIOMA COMANCHE,

ESCRITO POR EL SR. LIC.

D. Manuel Garcia Rejon,

Y DEDICADO A LA

SOCIEDAD MEXICANA
DE GEOGRAFIA Y ESTADISTICA.

MEXICO.
IMPRENTA DE IGNACIO CUMPLIDO,
Calle de los Rebeldes número 2.

1866.

Title page of García Rejón's Comanche vocabulary,
reproduced from the 1866 reprint.

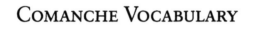

COMANCHE VOCABULARY

TEXAS ARCHAEOLOGY AND ETHNOHISTORY SERIES

Thomas R. Hester, Editor

COMANCHE VOCABULARY
TRILINGUAL EDITION

Compiled by
Manuel García Rejón

Translated and edited by
Daniel J. Gelo

UNIVERSITY OF TEXAS PRESS, AUSTIN

First edition, 1995

Requests for permission to reproduce material from this work
should be sent to Permissions, University of Texas Press, Box 7819,
Austin, TX 78713-7819.

∞ The paper used in this publication meets the minimum requirements of
American National Standard for Information Sciences—
Permanence of Paper for Printed Library Materials, ANSI Z39.48-1984.

LIBRARY OF CONGRESS CATALOGING-IN-PUBLICATION DATA

García Rejón, Manuel, 1819–1864.
    [Vocabulario del idioma comanche. English]
    Comanche vocabulary / compiled by Manuel García Rejón ; translated
and edited by Daniel J. Gelo. — Trilingual ed., 1st ed.
       p.   cm. — (Texas archaeology and ethnohistory series)
    Vocabulary lists in English, Comanche, and Spanish; text in English,
translated from the original Spanish.
    Includes bibliographical references.

    ISBN 0-292-72783-6 (pbk. : alk. paper)

    1. Comanche language—Dictionaries—Polyglot. 2. Dictionaries,
Polyglot. I. Gelo, Daniel J., date. II. Title. III. Series.
PM921.Z5G37 1995
497'.45—dc20   95-7813

FOR TERENCE AND THOMAS

CONTENTS

FOREWORD

This volume represents an important contribution to the ethnology of the Comanches. Intensive scholarship on the part of Dr. Daniel J. Gelo, an anthropologist on the faculty at the University of Texas at San Antonio, has provided researchers with an extensive Comanche vocabulary. This book was originally published in Mexico in the 1860s but has been both obscure and relatively inaccessible. Thus, Dr. Gelo's translation and accompanying annotations will make this significant document broadly available to ethnohistorians, linguists, and anthropologists who work with Comanche and other Southern Plains Native Americans.

Indeed, scholars from these and other disciplines will find the García Rejón vocabulary to be a source on many aspects of the lifeway of the Comanche people and the environment within which they lived. The dating of this vocabulary to the mid-nineteenth century allows evaluation and measurement of Comanche linguistic acculturation. For example, Dr. Gelo notes religious and symbolic terms found in this vocabulary but no longer present in contemporary Comanche language. The vocabulary also reflects the wide range of Comanche activity in Texas and northeastern Mexico, especially their raids into Mexico during this period. All sorts of information on the use of domestic animals, the role of hunting and gathering, and the range of certain mammalian species can be obtained from the vocabulary.

Perhaps of greatest interest to archaeologists is the information on Comanche pictography. García Rejón provides data on the practice of using animal scapulas for pictographic writing. Dr. Gelo has related the styles to the archaeological record of Historic pictographs in Texas and ventures to link some of these to the Comanches. The data on scapula writing and rock art suggest a "uniform pictography," as Dr. Gelo puts it, for the Comanches. This can hopefully be elaborated and enhanced by archaeologists working with such rock art sites.

I am grateful to Dan Gelo for bringing this manuscript to my attention so that it could be included in the Texas Archaeology and Ethnohistory Series. In addition, my thanks to Professor Brian Stross and Professor Emeritus T. N. Campbell of the Department of Anthropology, the University of Texas at Austin, for their assistance and advice.

Thomas R. Hester

EDITOR'S
INTRODUCTION

Manuel García Rejón's vocabulary of the Comanche language (García Rejón 1865) is by far the most extensive of those collected prior to the establishment of the Kiowa-Comanche-Apache Reservation in 1867, and it remains an outstanding resource for Uto-Aztecan linguists and those interested in Comanche culture. It offers several terms not documented anywhere else, as well as insight into phonological evolution, semantic replacement, and neologism; these features in turn can further an understanding of historical processes at work during the period. The vocabulary also includes information on pictography, preserving a rare sample of Comanche scapula drawing. At another level, García Rejón's work is important as an example of the scholarship that blossomed in Mexico during the Reform era even in the shadow of Indian depredations on the northern frontier. Despite the potential it holds for a variety of researchers, the document has seldom been utilized. The present edition, drawn from a copy of the 1866 reprint in the Benson Latin American Collection of the University of Texas at Austin, is intended to make the work more useful to modern readers by providing an English translation, by arranging the entries alphabetically, by noting and correcting errors in the original work (without deleting García Rejón's original information), and by annotating the material in the light of current knowledge of Comanche language and culture.

Manuel García Rejón y Mazo was not a trained linguist or lexicographer in the modern sense but a man of letters with an active intellect and a talent for capitalizing on the circumstances around him. Born in Mérida, Yucatán, in 1819 and educated in Mexico City, García Rejón had a career as an attorney, writer, and radical politician when these professions were particularly risky (Alvarez 1971; *Diccionario Porrua* 1976b; Cavazos Garza 1984). He held a judicial appointment in Monterrey as early as 1850, was suspended during the last reign of Santa Anna, but was reinstated in 1855. He became known for his anticlerical writings in *El Monitor Republicano* and his editorship of the equally liberal *Boletín Oficial* and was appointed secretary-general of Nuevo León under the caudillo Santiago Vidaurri, whom he had ardently supported in print. When not occupied with administrative matters, García Rejón took advantage of his position and travels through Mexico and South Texas to investigate regional history and culture, publishing records of Monterrey and studies of the Mayas as well as his own periodical, *Revista de Nuevo León y Coahuila.* This activity reflects a philosophical stance shared with more famous liberal compatriots such as Melchor Ocampo and Santos Degollado, scholar-statesmen who saw nativist literary and scientific efforts, including the study of Indian languages, as critical to the construction of a distinct Mexican national identity.

After Vidaurri was deposed by Benito Juárez in March 1864, García Rejón fled to Texas, but Union General Francis Herron turned him over to the centralists in Matamoros, and he was executed by a firing squad in late April. He left behind a manuscript for the present Comanche vocabulary, dedicated to the Sociedad Mexicana de Geografía y Estadística. (This prestigious order listed García Rejón as a corresponding member, and his father, Joaquín García Rejón y Carvajal [1784–1878], served there as an editor.) It fell to one Jesús Aguilar of Monterrey, who apparently replaced García Rejón as regional correspondent, to submit the document to the Sociedad for publication (Arroyo 1865, 1866; *Diccionario Porrua* 1976a, 1976b).

Here García Rejón's Comanche discoveries were approved by the noted philologist Francisco Pimentel (1832–1893), and consequently the vocabulary formed the basis for a discussion of Comanche in Pimentel's monumental *Lenguas indígenas de México* (1862–1865, 1874–1875), with much of García Rejón's manuscript reproduced verbatim or with minor improvements. Given this reliance on García

Rejón, Pimentel's evaluation of the *Vocabulario*, included as a fore-word in the published work, sounds patronizing, although his status as a full member of the society and role as referee would have de-manded a superior tone. With Pimentel's endorsement and, presum-ably, support from the author's grieving father, the vocabulary ap-peared as the last item in the society's bulletin for 1865 and was reprinted in pamphlet form soon after.

García Rejón's main consultant for the vocabulary, a Mexican named Andrés who was captured as a child and raised by the Coman-ches, would have been born about 1844 and would have lived through a turbulent period in tribal history. The decade opened with the infamous Council House Fight in San Antonio and subsequent raids and battles throughout Texas and into Mexico (Viscaya Canales 1968; Brice 1987) and ended with the southern Comanches suffering outbreaks of smallpox and cholera introduced by the forty-niners passing through Texas. All during the 1840s, Comanches negotiated treaties with the Republic of Texas and the succeeding United States government, as well as with German settlers in central Texas, but these agreements had no comprehensive effect (Kavanagh 1986; Schilz and Schilz 1989).

Comanche depredations in Texas increased nearly every year in the 1850s as the pressure of white settlement bore on the Indians and the federal government vacillated in its commitment to man a string of frontier forts (Tate 1971:43–47). In 1854 legislation was passed en-abling the establishment of the first Comanche reservation, the Clear Fork Comanche Reserve, comprising four leagues on the Clear Fork of the Brazos at the present boundary of Haskell and Throckmorton Counties, two hundred and forty miles north-northwest of San An-tonio de Béxar. An average of four hundred Penateka (García Rejón's Penande), less than half that division, occupied the site after 1855, but because of continued hostilities in the region, the reservation was abandoned in 1859, and the residents removed to the Leased District, now western Oklahoma (Richardson 1933:211–259). In his over-view of the tribe, García Rejón mentions the reservation but appar-ently did not know of its closing.

The remaining Penatekas and members of the other Comanche di-visions—Kotsoteka, Nokoni, Tenewa, Yamparika—still epitomized the free-ranging Plains Indian way of life, camping and hunting buffalo in a core area of western Oklahoma and northwestern Texas, trading across the Plains, and raiding for horses and cattle as far south as Durango. Thus García Rejón's main consultant and a second one, an anonymous female Comanche, were found in the eastern reaches of the Bolsón de Mapimí in extreme west-central Coahuila (García Rejón's "Paila"). This arid basin and range country was the southern terminus of the Chisos raiding trail and a favorite staging area for Apache and Comanche marauders in Mexico (Richardson 1933: 193–205; Smith 1959, 1960, 1961, 1963, 1970; Campbell and Field 1968; Tate 1971:46). Water was available in a string of marshy lakes on the eastern fringe of the depression; the Sierra Mojada proper and neighboring ranges offered protected positions. Apaches, mainly Lipans and Mescaleros, began launching attacks on settlements from the area around 1750 (Jones 1988:125), and troops were deployed against them systematically by 1778 (Thomas 1941:118). Comanches followed suit after 1780 and continued well into the next century. Today a number of toponyms in the region refer to the Apaches, and a small habitation in the Sierra Mojada is called El Comanche.

Comanche attacks in Mexico came most intensively during 1848–1852 and continued through the 1850s (Richardson 1933:201 ff.; Kavanagh 1986:130 ff.). Mexican settlers and errant Apaches alike were subject to massive theft and slaughter, and several towns in the Bolsón de Mapimí had to be abandoned. At least one hacienda resorted to paying protection on a regular basis in the form of livestock (Smith 1970). Thanks to a concerted reaction by Mexican patrols, assisted by mercenary scalp hunters, and stronger U.S. attempts to interrupt north-south Indian traffic, attacks beyond the Rio Grande declined markedly by 1860.

García Rejón's discussion of Captain Ugartechea's Comanche encounter in the late spring of 1861, however, shows that raids into Mexico did not cease entirely. It appears that the Comanches, ever opportunistic, were attuned to local troop movements and took immediate advantage when Federal forces withdrew from the Texas frontier for Civil War duty. In February 1861, Colonel Robert E. Lee resigned his command of Fort Mason, and seventeen other Federal installations were turned over to Texas that month (Conger et al. 1966:68, 165). The posts were deserted or occupied intermittently by Confederate volunteers. In August two ambitious but ineffective treaties were struck between the Comanches and the Confederate government (Richardson 1933:267 ff.).

García Rejón seems to suggest that his redeemed captive returned to the Mexican settlements of his own accord, or perhaps he was stranded. In any event, Andrés would have been thoroughly acculturated to Indian life, the typical fate of young male prisoners fortunate enough to survive the early stages of their captivity; indeed, it is well known that many boy prisoners grew to prominence as warriors and tribal civic leaders (see Corwin 1959; Greene 1972). The band affiliation of either consultant is, unfortunately, impossible to determine. Members of all the major divisions were active in Mexican raiding at this relatively late date. Efforts to detect a pattern of evidence for band dialect in the vocabulary were fruitless. The terms are not attributed to one or another of the consultants, and it is not known whether one or two dialects are represented. Even if these problems could be reasoned away, the current documentation of dialectal variation in Comanche (Wistrand-Robinson and Armagost 1990) is not thorough enough to support conclusions about the *Vocabulario*.

Whatever their lesser affiliation, García Rejón's associates represent an ethnic unit whose career has been a grand natural experiment in cultural persistence and change. Their language is the most easterly and most recent offshoot of the Numic branch of Uto-Aztecan, a language family widely represented in Mexico and the western United States. Comanche stands in comparison to related tongues such as Nahuatl, Hopi, Paiute, and particularly Shoshone, for the Comanches broke away from the Shoshones, perhaps around A.D. 1600, and left the intermontane west for the Plains, where they became the Uto-Aztecan speakers most committed to living as horse Indians.

Comanche and Shoshone are still so similar that the two have been classified as dialects of the same language (e.g., Miller 1972:3). But at least since the lifetime of García Rejón's consultants, the two dialects have evolved independently in different environments. (For preliminary discussion of the Shoshone-Comanche dialect chain and related issues of time depth, see Shaul 1981, 1986.) Occasionally García Rejón reports a term in 1860s Comanche that is absent from modern Comanche but present in modern Shoshone, while several other terms he gives appear to be unique to Comanche. Within Comanche, comparisons of word lists from different time periods are profitable, showing the variability of the language and creativity of its speakers, as well as the dynamic character of the Plains environment. García Rejón's document must figure prominently in all such questions of historical linguistics.

Several Spanish and English loanwords surface in the vocabulary as solid evidence of linguistic acculturation (cf. Shimkin 1980; Shaul 1981; Wistrand-Robinson and Armagost 1990). The commercial thrust of the interaction between Indians and non-Indians is indicated in these terms for cultivated plant foods, livestock, dry goods, and metal: *pijura* (*frijole*), *ecahchire* (*eka-*, "red" + *chili*), *muviporo* (pig; *mubi*, "nose" + *puerca*), *supereyos* (hat; *sombrero*), *pínica* (petticoat), and *póro* (bar [of iron]; *barra*). The *Vocabulario* is also replete with native terms for the objects that most frequently appear on lists of Spanish, Anglo-Texan, and U.S. gift and annuity goods from 1785 to 1867 (as compiled by Kavanagh 1986:310–350). The Comanche words for "awl," "bead," "bell," "red blanket," "white blanket," "cassock," "comb," "mirror," "white flag," "saltpeter," "scissors," "(fire) steel," and "vermilion," along with the aforementioned "hat" and "iron bar," are all conspicuous in view of the commodity lists. On the other hand, García Rejón's consultant(s) gave the same word for "ceiling" and "door," exhibiting a reluctance to contemplate anything other than a conical house. But in general the linguistic picture is of a society that moved rapidly and confidently into the Spanish and then U.S. mercantile spheres.

Most intriguing in this regard is the appearance of a specific term for "mustang," *cobé*; the word appears in only one other Comanche word list and persists only as the name of Kobi or Wild Horse, the Kwahadi headman who visited Washington in June 1880 (Berghaus 1851:52; Mallery 1881:406; Wallace and Hoebel 1952:281; Anonymous 1959). Given the central importance of the horse in Comanche culture, it is not surprising to find a monolexeme equivalent to "wild horse"; *cobé* supplements *tihïya*, "horse," from the Shoshone term for "cervine animal," and *puki*, "one's personal horse," originally "pet," as well as a host of descriptive terms referring to age, sex, coat color, and pattern (e.g., Wallace and Hoebel 1952:46). The derivation of *cobé* is not apparent, however, and the word faded from use as wild horses became increasingly less important in the Comanche economy. In 1834 frontier artist George Catlin sketched and painted memorable images of Comanches roping mustangs, and Catlin himself killed a wild horse while trying to "crease" it (stun it with a shot grazing the neck) (Catlin 1973:57–60), but already market forces were in place to encourage the Comanches to abandon such inefficient practices and concentrate on stealing domesticated animals. Westward-bound settlers were poised in Missouri, awaiting Mexican horses supplied by various Indian and white "entrepreneurs" (Flores 1991). Undoubtedly, too, the incipient Comanche class system, with its emphasis on power (*puha*), respect (*mabitsia*), and evidential material wealth, encouraged the more productive horse raiding over wild horse capture. Competition from the Cheyennes and other later arrivals would also have accelerated the shift. By 1875, when the last Comanche holdouts—some under Wild Horse himself—surrendered and settled on the Kiowa-Comanche-Apache Reservation and the patient study of the language could begin, mustanging was part of the Comanche past. The leader's death in 1891 may have further promoted loss of the word, as there was a taboo against speaking the names of the dead. The term *cobé* became so obscure that in 1959 one Comanche reported the spurious back-formation *Wye-Hoss* as the chief's Indian name (Anonymous 1959:61).

Numerous other animal terms are mentioned in the vocabulary, suggesting that most traditional hunting and gathering practices remained essential. The term for buffalo, *cuhtz*, today means "cow" unless modified with the prefix *nimi-*, "Indian," but García Rejón's consultants did not feel it was necessary to qualify the term; buffaloes were still the primary source of meat, even if (Flores 1991) the demise of the species was already imminent. The alien domesticates are named—cattle, pig, sheep, burro, rooster, chicken, turkey, cat— though it can be presumed that these animals were derided as inferior creatures much as they are today. The inclusion of "jaguar" will surprise those who know only its present range; jaguars were once more common north of the Rio Grande, and Dolly Webster, held captive by a Comanche party moving through the Texas Hill Country in 1837, mentions the "leopard cat" besides the wild cat and panther and relates two near-attacks by large felines (Dolbeare 1986:13–15). Alligators also had a more northerly range and would in any event have been known from forays to the Nueces River and coastal Texas (cf. Sowell 1884:207–208; Bollaert 1956:371, 373; Rister 1989:125).

On the other hand, the southern extent of the porcupine is often underestimated, but this animal was useful in Comanche medicine practice (McAllester 1940) and is named here.

Of all subjects in Comanche animal nomenclature, the bear is the most complicated, with numerous alternate terms, including at least one that is gender-specific, and some applied to other animals as well (Gelo 1989a). García Rejón compounds the matter with an otherwise unreported black bear term, *tunayó*. It can be speculated that because bear terms were common in proper names (the bear being symbolic of strength and invulnerability), alternate terms were promoted under the taboo of speaking the names of the dead. And following from the notion that it was disrespectful to use a person's name freely, alternate terms were spoken as euphemisms to avoid angering spirit bears. The *Vocabulario* also confirms the implication of captive Rachel Plummer, held during 1836–1838, that Comanches recognized a white bear as a distinct species (Plummer 1977:13). Judging from her discussion, this appears to have been the female grizzly; however, the word given by García Rejón, *tosagüera*, contains an element that once meant "male bear" but now is used for "mountain lion"! Moreover, García Rejón's word for "javelina" appears to be derived from "bear," in the manner that "horse" comes from the Shoshone "deer." Further study is needed to explain these instances of semantic replacement and to clarify Comanche ideas about bear taxonomy.

Among the other animals defined are the bullfrog, cougar, coyote, deer (two kinds recognized), dog, frog, jackrabbit, otter (homonymous with "hair wrapper" because braids were wrapped with strips of fur), (cottontail) rabbit, skunk (two terms), water snake, toad, wildcat (bobcat), and wolf. Birds named include the cardinal, crow, crane, duck, eagle, heron, kite, owl, partridge, roadrunner, turkey vulture, and woodpecker. Insects are also mentioned, notably the bee ("sugar store") and tarantula, whose name, *tapuêretz* (literally, "our hairy brother-in-law"), is equally revealing about Comanche attitudes toward spiders and affines. A similar review of plant names in the vocabulary can be conducted, engendering a fine sense of the Comanche's natural environment, subsistence practices, and notions of classification.

Some light is also shed on Comanche supernaturalism during the period. Two names are provided for the Great Spirit, the usual *taah-*

pue ("our father") and also *tatoco* ("our maternal grandfather"). This second term, not in use anymore, widens our sense of the creator being's personality, for while in Comanche social classification the father was a procreating figure but somewhat detached from the everyday affairs of his children (e.g., Gladwin 1948:83), the maternal grandfather was a favorite relative and tutor (e.g., Wallace and Hoebel 1952:126–127); the closeness expected of a maternal grandfather and grandson was signified by their use of a reciprocal kin term, and their relation was characterized by "indulgence and congeniality linked with the less severe forms of authority-obedience" (ibid.: 126). Furthermore, "the grandfather taught the grandson . . . the secrets of the hunt and the trail" (ibid.). Any metaphoric characterization of the Great Spirit as a matrilineal mentor appears to be lost today.

Also obsolete is the image of the Big Dipper as a rabbit (*tábo*); this survival is from Numic mythology, in which the rabbit is a trickster who arranges the alternation of day and night by fighting the sun and advocating a time for sleep and dreaming (e.g., Fowler and Fowler 1971:227–229). The morning star and Pleiades are named, the former prominent today in peyote cult iconography, the latter the subject of a frequently heard origin myth (e.g., St. Clair and Lowie 1909: 282). The mythic thunderbird appears as, literally, "sky-talker," one of numerous allusions in Comanche belief to speech as a manifestation of supernatural power; García Rejón describes a huge bird with burning wings whose cry is thunder. This is the first mention in print of Comanche belief in the widespread Plains spirit, significantly earlier than Mooney's (1896:968–969), which also implies the burning wings motif. A colorful description of the ogre *piamupitz* is also furnished. García Rejón tells us the being is a cannibalistic giant in human form who dwells in caves in mountains far to the north and carries a huge staff of wood; "they believe that when he breaks the staff, they die." This last detail is unique to García Rejón's account. Usually the creature is imagined as an owl (e.g., St. Clair and Lowie 1909: 275–276; Barnard 1941:115–116, 119–121). Its house was localized, via oral tradition, as Bat Cave in the Elk Range of the Wichita Mountains, north of Indiahoma, Oklahoma (cf. Barnard 1941:119; Wallace and Hoebel 1952:124).

Yet another notable datum is the homonymic relationship between the terms for "flower" and "foam of water": both are *sahtotzip*. It is likely that this connection is a vestige of a comprehensive Uto-Aztecan system of chromatic symbolism (Hill 1992) in which flowers, feathers, foam, fire, and butterflies appear in strings of metaphors evoking spiritual power. "The Flower World complex is only partially attested to on the margins of the Uto-Aztecan world in Takic and Numic languages" (ibid.:137); however, in 1989 I documented a germane Comanche procedure in which the eagle feathers from the headdress and dance bustle of a deceased man were disposed of by his widow, herself a renowned medicine woman (Gelo 1989b). She selected one of the places northeast of Fletcher, Oklahoma, where a plank bridge spans the Little Washita River. This creek is very placid, but here it broke over some rocks and logs downstream of the bridge, creating a dirty froth. When we got out of the car, the woman inspected the site and remarked on the foaming, and then carefully dropped the feathers, to the accompaniment of praying, so that they landed and floated away amid the foam. We waited anxiously to make sure none of the feathers became stuck on debris, and the procedure was over when the feathers and foam had drifted from sight. The role of flowing water as a desacralizing agent in Comanche and the use of local streams to dispose of old ritual objects are well known (e.g., Jones 1972, 1980), yet in this case the attention to foam, which at first seems inconsistent aesthetically with notions of purification, was a significant element in the procedure. Linguistic and ethnographic observations of this kind are crucial in determining the extent to which Comanche religion on the Plains is grounded in a larger Numic or Uto-Aztecan ethos (Gelo 1993:78–80).

More of Comanche symbolism and aesthetic is illuminated by García Rejón's information on scapula writing. Comanche use of an animal shoulder blade as a tablet for pictographs is also noted in Schoolcraft (1851–1857:4:253, 5:70; reproduced in Mallery 1893:206). Interpretation of the present pictographs must rest on the assumption that they were copied precisely by the author's associate Ugartechea and that they were reproduced as copied. While the depiction of the Indian bodies shows the insinuation of European style, the detail included on the shields suggests that some effort was made to furnish an accurate reproduction. It appears that the spatial relations between the elements are not retained except for a division of two "panels," one describing the Indians and the other, the Mexican force. Relatedly, no order of episode is indicated. Regardless of possible rearranging that would have eliminated narrative sequence, it seems clear that the scapula record was mainly enumerative and intended as a transitory account of military intelligence. In this general purpose, it resembles the Tally Sheet, an eighteenth-century Comanche document concerning a Comanche-Spanish battle against the Apaches, which was shown by Thomas (1929) to contain detailed information about the campaign.

Certain conventions of the Early and Late Biographic styles of rock art (Keyser 1987) are recognizable in the scapula, notably those common to both rock art and other pictorial works such as skin paintings and ledger books. The designation of non-Indians with brimmed hats is a standard practice and appears to be an extension of the concept of representing tribal affiliation by detailing hairstyle. A W. S. Soule photograph of Sun Boy (Mayhall 1962:117) shows the Kiowa in a brimmed hat and suggests the interest held by the Indians in such headgear. The three headless figures evince the Plains convention of signifying war fatality with decapitation (e.g., Mallery 1893:564–565; Cárdenas 1977, 1978), but they are also remindful that Mexican bounty laws promoted beheading of Indian raiders (e.g., Smith 1960, 1970, 1973). The shields with personal designs serve as glyphs for two of the dead Indians, while the rifles above heads are a common device for indicating strength of the enemy. The absence of horses or the customary horseshoe symbol is peculiar and, along with the caption "pisadas de Indios," suggests that the Comanche party was traveling locally on foot.

The scapula bears closer comparison with Comanche rock art as far as it can be identified. In his excellent article urging the coordinated interpretation of historic rock art and Plains Indian portable pictorial art, Parsons (1987) details two Texas Panhandle sites of probable Comanche execution that contain ideographs used on the García Rejón scapula. The Mujares (Mojares, Mujeres) Creek petroglyphs in Oldham County use the rifle device, albeit with more detail suggesting a flintlock; petroglyphs at the Verbena Site in Garza County show stock-and-barrel rifle signs as well as short horizontal lines indicating human footprints. Such similarities with the scapula "dispatch" support Parsons's thesis that the petroglyphs record important battles.

A possible Comanche attribution is also given to the historic petroglyphs at Chimney Rock in the Panhandle (Kirkland and Newcomb
1967:212–214), one of which (ibid.: 214, Plate 159, No. 12) contains a shield with a four-armed star design remarkably similar to
García Rejón's first shield. The realistic human forms at this site are
also reminiscent of those on García Rejón's scapula. Other likely Comanche sites with hatted figures include Marfa Lake Shelter (ibid.:
127–129), Moran Shelter (ibid.: 170–171), Hueco Tanks (ibid.: 173
ff.), Vaquero Shelter in Pressa Canyon (Turpin 1982:39, 77–80,
among others), the Hussie Miers Site—this an obvious combat autobiography showing spiked helmets and rifles (Turpin 1989), and
Frio Canyon, with its celebrated rifle-toting "Fighting Parson" figure
(Jackson 1938:247–249; Kirkland and Newcomb 1967:12, 50–51,
160–161), all in Texas. Thus García Rejón's scapula information
gives further evidence of a uniform pictography and so helps advance
understanding of Comanche symbolism and ethnohistory.

Returning to linguistics, García Rejón displays some natural talent
for description and analysis. He fails to give a roster of phonemes at
the outset, but his phonology based on the Spanish sound system usually works well in reflecting pronunciation, and he accounts in his
opening remarks for gradation in the pronunciation of certain con-
sonants. Some notice is given to voiceless vowels and the phonemic
glottal stop via the use of a circumflexed *e*, though García Rejón is
unsophisticated in his treatment of these elements. Imprecisions in the
recording of vowels are not always consequential, however, since
"the distinction between vowels such as /a/ vs. /[ï]/ and /o/ vs. /u/ is
often reduced or lost phonetically" by Comanche speakers (Wistrand-
Robinson and Armagost 1990:239; cf. Miller 1972:16). García Rejón also shows a grasp of Comanche morphology with his analysis of
prefixes and postfixes and the intensifier *tibitzi* (*tibitsi*), and the fre-
quency of compounding in the language, later recognized as an important characteristic (e.g., Becker 1931, 1936; Osborn and Smalley
1949; Shimkin 1980) is clear from his discussion.

Beyond the documentation of grammatical details, García Rejón
compiled a rich lexicon of over eight hundred terms, testimony to the
rapport he was able to build with his consultants. Unfortunately, his
elicitation techniques are not recorded in detail, but it is clear that he
was showing his consultants objects from his Monterrey surround-

ings, and probably pictures as well. There are several terms for household items, ranch equipment, a reference to bullfighting, and even a word for stilts (*júmia*, "stick-walk," perhaps an offhand neologism). The inclusion of a term for guards reminds us that the author's sources had until recently been held as prisoners. And when collecting body part terms, García Rejón obviously pointed to his consultant, since the pronoun "my" (*nï*) is included accidentally with the term for "clavicle" (see below).

Many important aspects of García Rejón's work are not highlighted by the author. He does not point out the loanwords from Spanish and English, if indeed he recognized them. Nor does he distinguish between obvious neologisms and older Comanche words. In some cases, García Rejón fails to recognize homonyms (e.g., *nojitó*, "play," *nohito*, "deceive"), and sometimes he renders the same element with different spellings (e.g., *tetza* vs. *tsa*, *nacútusí* vs. *nacutzi*, *supereyos* vs. *superellos*) as if he has forgotten his own orthographic conventions. The significant homonymic relationship between "flower" and "foam of water" is overlooked.

These shortcomings are not a problem for the aware reader, but some others—outright mistakes—can easily lead to confusion. There are consistent errors that appear to be typographic: *n* for *u* or *w*, *r* for *z*, *e* for *c*; these mistakes may be obvious only to those who already know Comanche. Moreover, the Comanche-Spanish section of the original vocabulary is not an exact reversal of the Spanish-Comanche section; many entries in the Spanish-Comanche section are absent from the other, and some in the second section do not appear in the first. In several cases, entries found in both sections vary in spelling or definition. (These discrepancies between the first and second sections suggest strongly that the sections were taken down independently of one another, possibly one each from the two consultants.) Such problems lessen the utility of the original document, as does the fact that the entries in the original are not fully alphabetized, only listed under initial letter.

In the present edition the original Spanish is reproduced, though the entries have been alphabetized and standardized, and the original first and second sections have been brought into concordance. (Terms and entries that did not originally appear in a section are marked with an asterisk.) García Rejón's Spanish regionalisms and variant spellings are clarified, and diacritics have been added where missing from the original. His discussion of tenses ("Brief Page on What Is Found within the Vocabulary"), which appears at the end of the original document, is here placed ahead of the entries. Also, the first section has been expanded to include comparative material from later word lists. For this purpose Wistrand-Robinson and Armagost (1990) is cited when possible because it is the most recent and comprehensive work, superseding Canonge (1958), and because it employs an orthography used by several linguists working in Comanche (for the back unrounded vowel, /i/ has been substituted for Wistrand-Robinson's /ʉ/; for the glottal, /ʔ/ instead of /ʔ/; and voiceless vowels are italicized, out of typographic convenience). Comparative material is also drawn from Berghaus (1851), Gatschet (1884), Detrich (1894, 1895), Carlson and Jones (1939), McAllester (1940), Gladwin (1948), Wallace and Hoebel (1952), Fowler and Fowler (1971), Miller (1972), and Crapo (1976). These sources are abbreviated in the entries as Wi, Be, Ga, De94, De95, CJ, Mc, Gl, WH, Fo, Mi, and Cr, respectively. No effort was made to find cognates or suggest etymologies beyond Comanche and Shoshone, but those who wish to do so can begin with Sapir's *Southern Paiute Dictionary* (1931). Problematic Comanche terms were reviewed by the editor with Mrs. Margaret Thomas (Wahaper Wahnee), a seventy-year-old native Comanche speaker and daughter of the late Mary Wahkinney, an associate in the research of Wistrand-Robinson and Armagost.

Thanks are owed to Margaret Thomas for her patient discussion of the definitions provided here and for many hours of tutoring me in the Comanche language since 1982. Series editor Thomas R. Hester merits my deepest admiration for his ability to see the potential of this volume and my deepest gratitude for his advice in revising and publishing it. Robert M. Hill II helped with specific questions of Spanish usage and rendered a parallel translation of García Rejón's introductory comments that revealed faults in my own draft. T. N. Campbell, Gerald Poyo, and Brian Stross recommended several improvements. Important bibliographic and historical information was shared by Adán Benavides, Oakah Jones, and Bruce Shackleford. Kim Sayre identified several of the cognate terms from other word lists and entered them in the manuscript. Raymond R. Baird, James A. Goss,

Jane H. Hill, Elizabeth A. H. John, David P. McAllester, and William K. Powers provided tangible and intangible encouragements. My sincere appreciation is extended to each of these people. The translation was prepared with the aid of a Faculty Research Award from the University of Texas at San Antonio, receipt of which is gratefully acknowledged.

Daniel J. Gelo

VOCABULARY OF THE COMANCHE LANGUAGE

OPINION

In fulfillment of the commission that it pleased the vice president to give me, that I examine a manuscript vocabulary of the Comanche language, written by Sr. García Rejón, and dedicated by its author to this Society, I proceed to manifest the judgment I have formed of the aforementioned work.

The author begins by presenting a sample of hieroglyphic writing, used by the Comanches, that pertains to our epoch, referring to a battle that the Indians had with the Mexican commandant Ugartechea. This sample of writing is precisely of the *representative* genre, in which material things are copied and imitated; there is no *symbolic* sign, much less *phonetic*; the writing of the Comanches represents, then, the infancy of the art [of writing].

Before the dictionary, the author has put some grammatical observations on the language, which give some idea of it, but very imperfectly, since it explains nothing about the verb, the principal part of speech.

The Vocabulary contains, to my mind, all the words necessary to begin to speak the language and to initiate philological comparisons with the other Mexican languages. Reading over the pages of the dictionary, I have found various *primitive* words, entirely analogous to the Aztec or Mexican tongue, which force the presumption of a relationship between the two languages. However, this is a point that deserves rectification, and I shall do so in Volume 3 of my work on indigenous languages of Mexico.[1]

This suffices to indicate that the book of which I treat is not only curious, but useful, and its importance grows when one considers that there is no other, at least to my knowledge, on the Comanche language.

I think, then, that the work of Sr. Rejón should be printed as soon as possible in our *Bulletin,* and to this end I make a formal proposal, which I beg the Society to accept.

Mexico City, March 23, 1865—Francisco Pimentel.

PROLOGUE

On June 16, 1861, there arrived in this city, sent by the leading political authority of Cienegas,[2] a captive [male] youth of the Comanches, who had presented himself in that village. He appeared completely savage; he spoke no Spanish, and his age would be from sixteen to seventeen years. As it was not known what else to do with him, I asked the government that he be given to me to educate him and to see if he could be taught some trade.

In the beginning, the labor I had to understand him and get him to understand me was extraordinary because, reduced to captivity among the Comanches, as he explained to me, at a very young age, it was there that he began to speak, and he knew no other tongue than that of those savages.

Because of these difficulties, the idea came to me to make some notes on Comanche words in order to help my captive, and when he understood my objective, he formally undertook to teach me the names of all the things presented him, so that I should tell him its equivalent in Spanish; thus it is that what was at first a pastime for me later became my favorite occupation in the very short intervals of rest from the labors of my position as secretary of the government of this state.

The natural brilliance of my captive, the affection that he professes to me, and the repeated exercises we did inclined me to form a Vocabulary and to make the aforementioned observations.

Shortly before the arrival of this captive, the commandant Capt.

José María Ugartechea sent to this capital a [female] Comanche Indian, who he had made prisoner in an encounter he had in the desert; and thinking that it would serve me well to associate her with my work, I had her taken from the house of reclusion [jail or prison] in which she found herself, and with this assistant I rectified what I had learned from my captive.

I do not feel that I have made a finished work, but I have given beginning to an undertaking that another or others may finish, correcting the many errors that I must necessarily have committed.

I consider my work insignificant and shall be rewarded for it if it is received with kindness by the corporation to which it is dedicated.

Monterey [*sic*], etc.

To the Sociedad Mexicana de Geografía y Estadística, as proof of ad-miration and acknowledgment of the persistent eagerness with which it procures the advancement of Mexico, not only in the two important disciplines for which it is named, but wherever it extends its enlight-ened action and influence.

The Comanche nation, which is situated between the State of Texas and New Mexico, in United States territory, is composed of the fol-lowing tribes of peoples, to wit: Yaparehca, Cuhtzuteca, Penande, Pa-carabo, Caiguaras, Noconi or Yiuhta, Napuat or Quetahtore, Ya-paine, Muvinabore, Sianabore, Caigua, Sarritehca, and Quitzaene. All these tribes speak Comanche, but the last three also have private and distinct dialects.[3]

The Comanches form one of the savage nations of the North, and from among them loosen more or less numerous parties, which invade the territory of the Republic and make the devastating war of barbar-ians, or they occupy themselves in causing mischief in Texas.

The Americans have managed to reduce several hundred, particu-larly of the Penande, and they hold them in the neighborhood of Béjar at a place they call Reserve, but notwithstanding that which the gov-ernment spends to keep the peace and socialize these barbarians, they continue to make incursions, engaging in all the excesses to which they are accustomed.

The Comanches are completely savage, and though of a downcast aspect and appearing sluggish in their movements, they are very agile in the field and extremely skillful on horseback, surpassing in this ac-tivity all the other barbarians.

Their ideas are transmitted by means of hieroglyphics; I have had the fortune that there came into my possession a dispatch or warning that was given by some Indians to others, after they had been beaten by commandant Capt. José María Ugartechea, when he made a pris-oner of the [female] Indian I spoke of in the prologue. This message was found by my [male] captive on an expedition that he made to the Desert and in which he served as guide, in one of so many watering places in the Sierra Mojada; it was written on a horse scapula which the soldiers destroyed after the leader of the expedition copied it and the captive deciphered it. Here you have this notice with the respective explication:

On a horse scapula, they discovered drawn in pencil, at Segunda Agua, in the Paila, these hieroglyphs, September 7, 1861.

By the number of rifles and that of the dead Indians, it appears that the combat depicted on the scapula represents the encounter Ugartechea had with the barbarians last month, and according to the captive, it is a warning given by those who were in the Segunda Agua scouting party, and they left it to advise others that they should go and return to that place, thus like other signs that indicate this last.

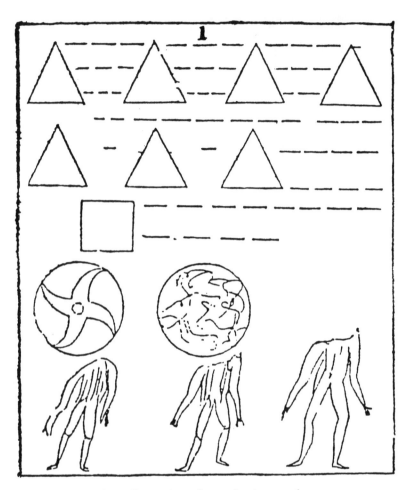

First illustration of scapula pictographs,
reproduced from the 1866 reprint.

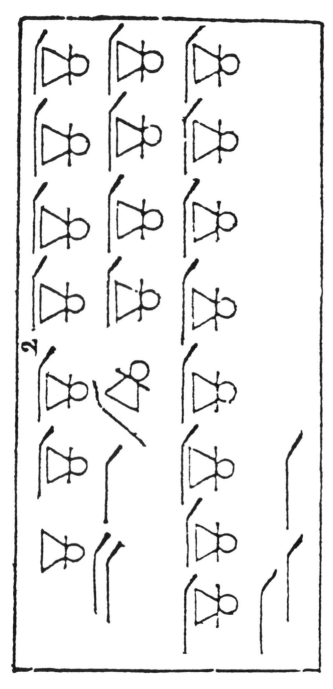

Second illustration of scapula pictographs, reproduced from the 1866 reprint.

Explanation which the captive
Andrés gave.

hut or house

house

footsteps of Indians that
left to fight

shields of the Indians that
died, which correspond to
two of the three bodies
depicted

soldiers

carbines

*Third illustration, a key to the pictographic
symbols, reproduced from the 1866 reprint.*

VARIOUS OBSERVATIONS

To be able to read the Comanche language one must bear in mind that the *h* should be aspirated softly. The *tz* should be pronounced by pressing the tip of the tongue against the upper teeth and emitting the breath forcefully. The *v* is pronounced as the Spaniards do. The double *r* is pronounced very softly; but if I have used it, it is to denote the difference of sound when one writes the simple [*r*]; the Spanish word *carrera* contains the two sounds of double and plain [*r*] in Comanche. The *r* at the beginning of speaking is pronounced softly. The *ê* with circumflex accent denotes that it should be pronounced like the French silent *e*.

There are various words that modify the meaning of those with which they are joined, and I consider it of the greatest importance to specify them.

The word *guaht*, which means "without," postfixed to another, expresses the absence of that which the other word signifies, for example, *moo* "hand," *mooguaht* "without hand."

The word *tibitzi*, which means "very," prefixed once to an adjective, forms the comparative; and if put twice it denotes the superlative, and if three or more [times], it carries the meaning of an extreme exaggeration in that which is expressed, for example *yup*, "fat"; *tibitzi yup*, "fatter"; *tibitzi tibitzi yup*, "most fat"; *tibitzi tibitzi tibitzi yup*, "very fattest," and so on.

Cuma is a contraction of the word *ucuma*, which means a male when discussing the sexes of animals, and postfixed to the noun determines the masculine sex; for example, *areca*, "deer"; *arecacuma*, "male deer."

Piab also is a contraction of the word *upiab*, which means a female, and postfixed to a noun determines the feminine sex; for example, *areca*, "deer"; *arecapiab*, "female deer."

Tua; this word means "son," and postfixed it carries the meaning of "offspring"; for example, *areca*, "deer"; *arecatua*, "the son or the offspring of the deer."

In Comanche there are three numbers to a noun: singular, dual, and plural.

The dual is formed by postfixing to the noun the particle *neuh*; for example, *areca*, "deer" [singular]; *arecaneuh*, "two deer."

The plural generally is formed by postfixing to the noun the particle *ne*; for example, *areca*, "deer" [singular]; *arecane*, "more than two deer" [plural].

There are various nouns with irregular plurals, and I identify these in the Vocabulary; for example, *pac*, "arrow"; *pacande*, "arrows."

The genitives of possession are expressed as in English, and generally between one and another noun, one interposes the particle *a*; for example, the tail of the horse *tehi a casi*, which translated literally is "of the horse the tail."

To express the trade or craft that one practices, they form a compound from the word that denotes that which one produces with said craft, or that specifies the thing which is worked upon, [and] from the expression *taibo*, which means "people," allowing in some cases a certain modification, concerning which I have not yet been able to establish a rule; thus, to say "cobbler," they form a compound of the word *nap*, which means "shoe," and the expression *taibo*, and they say *naparaibo*; to say "shepherd" they make a compound of *chiva*, "herd of goats," and of *taibo*; and say *chivaraibo*. In the Vocabulary, I have attempted to provide as many of these nouns as possible.

BRIEF
PAGE
ON WHAT IS FOUND WITHIN
THE VOCABULARY

TO BE — *TZA* OR *TZARÉ*

PRESENT[4]

I am: *ne tzaré*
you are: *en tzaré*
that is: *or tzaré*
we are: *nen tzaré*
you (plural) are: *muen tzaré*
those are: *ore tzaré*

To express this tense with negation, use the particle *que*, postfixed to the verb, thus: *ne tza que*: I am not.

PRETERIT IMPERFECT

I was: *ne tzaréja*
you were: *en tzaréja*
that was: *or tzaréja*, etc.

To express this tense with negation, use the particle *que* as in the preceding.

PRETERIT PERFECT

Omit the last syllable.

I was: *ne tza bues*
you were: *en tza bues*
that was: *or tza bues*, etc.

To express this tense with negation, use the particle *que* as in the preceding, omitting the previous *bues*, and the syllable *re*.

FUTURE

Add *né*, omitting the last syllable.

I will be: *ne tzaréno*
you will be: *en tzaréno*
that will be: *or tzaréno*, etc.

To express this tense with negation, use the particle *que* as in the present and the preterit imperfect.

ABBREVIATIONS USED

Be	Berghaus (1851)
CJ	Carlson and Jones (1939)
Cr	Crapo (1976)
De94	Detrich (1894)
De95	Detrich (1895)
Fo	Fowler and Fowler (1971)
Ga	Gatschet (1884)
Gl	Gladwin (1948)
Mc	McAllester (1940)
Mi	Miller (1972)
WH	Wallace and Hoebel (1952)
Wi	Wistrand-Robinson and Armagost (1990)
*	Denotes a term or entry found elsewhere in the original

ENGLISH-SPANISH-COMANCHE VOCABULARY

A

above [adj] {arriba} *mábat* [cf. paniput*i* maba?at*i*, high, tall (lit. "upward long") Wi 75]

ace [n] {as (de la baraja)} *cém* (the other cards up to the seven are assigned the name of the number they show) [cf. s*i*m*i*, one Wi 97; watas*i*, ace Wi 146]

acid indigestion [n] {acedia} *techiaroihp* [cf. t*i*k*i*, referring to food Wi 130]

Adam's apple [n] {nuez (de la garganta)} *maténicue* [cf. ni"-, pertaining to voice Cr 59]

afternoon [n] {tarde (la)} *yeihca* [cf. tabe *i*hy*i*ihka Wi 99]

air [n] {aire} *niet* [cf. n*i*et*i*, wind, breeze Wi 67]

all [numerical adj] {todo} *uacatz* [oyo?ko Wi 73]

alligator [n] {lagarto} *neneyeue* [n*i*n*i*?y*i*wi? Wi 69]

also [adv] {también} *sautzá* [error: *suatzá**; cf. t*i*as*i* Wi 127]

American [n] {Norteamericano} *pabotabeb* [cf. pabo taiboo?, white man Wi 73]

ankle [n] {tobillo} *míhtzi* [miihts*i* Wi 45]

ant [n] {hormiga} large red {grande, colorada} *anicútz;* small, called mantequera {pequeña, llamada mantequera} *anicúra* [an*i*kuura?, ant Wi 12]

anus [n] {ano} *taen* [cf. taina, hole Wi 102]

arm [n] {brazo} *puêr* [p*i*ira Wi 91]

armpit [n] {arca (del brazo)}

anaruhcat [anatukate   Wi
12]

arrow   [n]   {flecha}   *pac*
[paak*a*   Wi 73]; arrows
{flechas}   *pacandé*

arrowhead   [of flint]   [n]   {pe-
dernal (de la flecha)}   *tahc*
[tahka?   Wi 100]

arroyo, large   [n]   {arroyo
grande}, river   [n]   {río}   *piajunubi* [cf. pia, big   Wi 79;
hunu?b*i,* stream   Wi 20]

ash   [n]   {ceniza}   *etzip* [et*i*sip*i,*
ashes   Wi 17]

atole [corn porridge]   [n]
{atole}   *cahtzáp, cohtzap*

aunt   [n]   {tía}. The same as
mother   [*pia*]

autumn   [n]   first month {otoño
(primera luna)}   *tamasual*
[cf. tahma, spring season,
summer   Wi 101] *tocoeh-
catz** [error: *tocoehtatz*; cf.
tokwet*i,* exact, proper   Wi
109; taats*a,* summer season
Wi 99]; second month {otoño
(segundo luna)}   *equeromhcat** [cf. kwihne?, wintertime
Wi 38] *tocoehtatz* [cf. tokwet*i,* exact, proper   Wi 109;
taats*a,* summer season   Wi
99]; third month {otoño (tercera luna)}   *equeromhcal*
[error: *equeromhcat*; cf.
kwihne?, wintertime   Wi 38]
*tomohcat** [cf. tommo, winter, year   Mi 141]

awl   [n]   {alezna [lezna]}   *te-*

trahquená   [error: *tetzahquená**; cf. Widyu, Awl (band
name)   WH 27; Ditsikana,
Sewers (band name)   WH
27; t*i*tsahk*i*na?, sewing ma-
chine   Wi 138]

B

baby   [n]   {muchachito, niño}
[either sex]   *oná* [ohna?a?
Wi 71]

back   [n]   {espalda, lomo}   *jotoco* [ohutuk*i,* flank of animal   Wi 72; cf. "flank" below]

bag, cloth   [n]   {costal, ropero}
uanauósa; leather bag {costal
de istle ó de cuero}   *nárso*
[nar*i*so, bag, sack   Wi 58]

bald   [adj]   {calvo}   *papiguaht*
[cf. pahtsi bapikat*i,* bald
headed   Wi 74]

ball   [n]   {pelota}   *nasehpé*
[na?s*i*hpee   Wi 63]

bar (of iron)   [n]   {barra (de
hierro)}   *póro*

bark of trees   [n]   {corteza de
los palos}   *poap* [po?a?   Wi
85]

bat [animal]   [n]   {murciélago}
jonopitz [hono-pittseh   Mi
109]

bathe oneself   [v]   {bañarse}
pajabitó [pahabit*i*   Wi 74]

bead   [n]   {chaquira, avaloria
pequeño}   *choom* [tsoom*i*
Wi 122]

bean [n] {frijol} *pijura* [pih-úura   Wi 81]

bear [n] black bear {oso negro} *guasápe* [wasape, bear   Wi 146], *tunayó* [cf. tu-, black   Wi 123]; white bear {oso blanco} *tosagüera* [cf. tosa, white   Mi 142; wïra, male bear, obsolete, Mc; wïra?, panther, mountain lion   Wi 156]

beard [n] {barba (el bello de la cara)} *motz* [motso   Wi 46]

beaver [n] {castor} *pámouetz* [pa'uhmaa, waterbaby   Mi 124]

because [conj] {porque} *aui*

bed [n] {cama} *noróhnap* [norïnapï   Wi 66]

bedspread [n] {sobrecama} *sóna* [cf. soni, mattress; soni-ppeh, blanket   Mi 134]

bee, wasp [n] {abeja, avispa} *pinahuárami* [error: *pinah-nárami*; pihnaa?, sugar   Wi 81; narïmïï?, store   Wi 58]

before [adv] {antes} *nójo* [cf. ek'-ah-nah   De94 105]

belch [n] {eructo} *acuareit* [akwarïtï (v)   Wi 12]

bell [n] {campana} *cauojué* [kawohwï?   Wi 26]; tinkler (small bell) {cascabel} *oajuiauojué* [cf. oha-, prefix referring to yellow color   Wi 71; kawohwi?   Wi 26]

belly [n] {barriga} *pihpó* [pihpoo?, water jug (made of hide or animal stomach . . .)   Wi 81]

below [adj] {abajo} *maruhcát* [cf. tuhkatï, downward   Wi 123]

belt [n] {cinturón} *najoiquite* [cf. nehki?   Wi 63]

biceps [n] {lagartillo (del brazo)} *pueratzuqui* [cf. pïïra, arm   Wi 91]

big [adj] {grande} *piápre* [pia   Wi 79]

Big Dipper [n] {osa mayor (carro)} *tábo* [cf. tabu?-kina?, rabbit   Wi 100]

bird [n] {pájaro} *juhtzú* [huutsúu   Wi 21]; any small bird {pájaro pequeño (cualquier)} *tiriejuhtzú* [cf. tïe, small   Wi 128; huutsúu, bird   Wi 21]

bite [v] {morder} *quehtziaró* [kïhtsiarï   Wi 34]

black (the color) [adj] {negro (el color)} *tuhubit* [to'-hovit   De94 96]; black (pigmen.) [n] {negra (tinta)} *turuhpi* [cf. tu-, black   Wi 123; tïpi, rock   Wi 135]

blanket [n] red blanket {frazada colorada} *ecatzasabscá* [error: *ecatzasabocá**; echka-tatosawoka, *Rother Blankett* (red blanket)   Be 52]; white blanket {frazada blanca} *totzasabscá* [error: *tosasabocá**; cf. tosa-, white   Wi 110; echkatatosawoka,

Rother Blankett (red blanket) Be 52]

blind [adj] {ciego} *puiguat* [pui hwai Wi 88]

blood [n] {sangre} *puehpi* [pee"-pin Mi 129]

blue [adj] {azul} *evivit* [ebipit*i̵*, blue-gray, light blue Wi 14]

boil [v] {hervir} *noyaehbenit* [cf. no?yaik*i̵*t*i̵* Wi 66]

bone [n] {hueso} *tzuhuip* [error: *tzuhnip**; cf. tsuhni Wi 122]

bottle [n] {botella} *puihguioteauh*

bow (for arrow) [n] {arco (de la flecha)} *et* [eet*i̵* Wi 14]

boy [n] young boy {muchacho} *tuinéhpua* [tuin*i̵*hp*i̵*? Wi 124]; young boys {muchachos} *pihiande* [pihi?-an*ï̵* Wi 80]

bracelet [n] (of hide, for use with bow) {pulsera (de cuero para usar el arco)} *picamauitzohc* [pikamawitchoXk, wrist guard Ga 119]; bracelet (of metal) {pulsera (de metal)} *oajuimauitzohc* [cf. ohahpuhihwi, copper Wi 71; ma?witsohko, bracelet Wi 45]

brain [n] {cerebro} *cahpistoyopét*; brains {sesos} *ucubisi* [kub*i*si Wi 31]

brave [n] {valiente} *teconiuap* [tekw*i̵*niwap*i* Wi 107]

bread [n] {pan de harina} *têsahta* [cf. tohtía? Wi 108]

breast (woman's) [n] {pecho (la mama)} *pitzi* [pitsii? Wi 83]

breechcloth [n] {pampanilla} *tzanicá* [tson'-e-kah De94 82]

bridle [n] {freno} *arrae* [arai Wi 12–13]

brier [n] {tenaza (planta)} *tamutzoe* [tamutso?i, greenbrier Wi 103]

bring [v] {traer} *mayahque* [jaa-kii", bring here Cr 36]

brother (older brother) [n] {hermano (el mayor)} *bávi* [pabi? Wi 73]; (younger brother) {hermano (el menor)} *rámi* [tami? Wi 103]; older brother (my) {hermano mayor (mi)} *nebári* [error: *nebavi*; cf. *nebave**; n*i̵*, my Wi 67; pabi?, older brother Wi 73]; younger brother (my) {hermano menor (mi)} *nerámi* [cf. n*i̵*, my Wi 67; tami?, younger brother Wi 103]

brother-in-law, my (man speaking) [n] {cuñado (del hombre) mi} *neretz* [cf. n*i̵*, my Wi 67; tetsi, man's brother-in-law Wi 107]; my (woman speaking) {cuñado (de la mujer) mi} The same as **husband** [*cumahpue*].

brush (made from agave) [n]

{escobeta (peine de lechuguilla)} *natzistuya* [natzistuge, *Haarpinsel* (camel-hair brush) Be 52]

bucket [n] {caso de cobre} *uistúa* [wihtua? Wi 149]

buffalo [bison] [n] {cíbolo} *cuhtz* [nïmï kuhtsu? Wi 68; cf. kuhtsu? Wi 30]

bugle [n] {corneta o clarin} *piaguoin* [cf. pia-woinu, big horn, big bugle Wi 310; pia-woin, *Trompete* (trumpet) Be 53; Pi-ha-gwai-na, The drummer (*sic*, Washakie's name) Fo 269]

bullet [n] {bala} *nabac* [nabaak*a* Wi 49]

bullfrog [n] {tiburón (rana grande)} *murayáque* [ebimuura ya?ke? Wi 14]

bulrush, maguey stalk [n] {tule y también quiote} *pamoc* [error: *pamoe*; cf. pamu, watercress Mi 124; pa?mutsi, plant similar to water lily Wi 78]

burn [v] {quemar} *cuchtonaró* [kuts*i*tonarï Wi 32]

burro (male) [n] {burro (asno)} *cusiuibi* [kutsi?-wobi?, donkey Wi 32]; female {burra} *cusimúra* [kusimuura, donkey Wi 32]

butterfly [n] {mariposa} *ueyahcorá* [error: *ueyahcoró*;* we'-yáh-co-ro' De94 125]

buttock [n] {nalga} *pabohtoc* [pabo tuhku, hindquarter, light meat, thigh meat Wi 73]

button snakeroot [n] {poleo sylvestre} *atabitzanoyo** [atabitsïnoi Wi 13]

buy [v] {comprar} *temuecuató* [cf. tïmïïrï Wi 133]

C

cactus, desert Christmas, *Opuntia leptocaulis* DeCandolle [n] {tasajillo (planta)} *canauocué** [cf. kanah, thin Mi 111; wokwe, peyote Wi 150]

calf [body part] [n] {pantorrilla} *tauitz* [ta?wiits*a* Wi 106]

calm [adj] {sereno} nebaep

candle [n] {vela} *cupitá* [cf. kup*i*ta, lamp Wi 31; tosahtuka?, tosa yuhu rukai?, candle Wi 111]

canine tooth [n] {colmillo} *quêhtzi* [cf. kïïts*i*, wisdom tooth Wi 36]

carbine, rifle [n] {carabina, y también fusil} *piaet* [cf. pia, loud Wi 79; eetï, bow Wi 14; tawo?i?, rifle Wi 105; piai, *Gehehr* (*Feuer-*) (rifle) Be 53]

cardinal (bird) [n] {cardenal (ave)} *ecjuhtzú* [ek*a*huutsu? Wi 16]

carriage [n] {carro} *uóbipuc* [wobi puuk*u*, buggy, hack Wi 149]

carry [v] {llevar} *mayah-cuató* [cf. toyaakatï Wi 112]

cassock [n] {casaca y también frac} *pahcusó, paraibocusó* [cf. paraiboo?, chief Wi 76; kwasu?*u*, coat Wi 37]

cat [n] {gato} *uaó* [wa?oo? Wi 147]

cattle [n] {ganado vacuno} *pimoró* [pimoroo?, cow Wi 82]

ceiling [n] {techo} *namarema* [see **door**]

centipede [n] {cien pies} *soomó* [soo mo?o? Wi 95]

chameleon [n] {camaleón} *mahquitzaná* [cf. nak*i* toone, lizard Wi 52]

charge [make responsible for] [v] {encargar} *saitinereneyaquenoqui**

cheek [n] {cachete} *arrab* [cf. arap*i*, jaw Wi 13]

cheese [n] {queso} *pitzip-a-namarrivap* [cf. pitsipa, milk Wi 83; nahmuiH, moldy Mi 120]

chest [body part] [n] {pecho (el)} *nénap* [nïnap*ï* Wi 69]

chewing gum [n] {chitle [chicle]} *sanahcó* [cf. sanah-koo? kïtsïkwet*ï* Wi 91]

chical (green corn cooked and dried in the sun) [n] {chical (maize tierno cocido y secado al sol)} *cuasehani* [cf. kwa-sïtï, cook Wi 37; haníib*i*, corn Wi 18]

chicken [n] {gallina} *cocorá* [kokorá?a Wi 29]

chili [n] {chile (pimiento de la India)} *ecahchire* [ekatsiira?, red pepper Wi 15]

chin [n] {barba (parte de la cara)} *páretz* [parïitsi Wi 76]

church [n] {iglesia (templo)} *puácane* [puha kahni Wi 86]

clavicle [n] {clavícula (la)} *nejuhcutaen* [cf. nï, my Wi 67; huuk*u*, collarbone Wi 20]

clean [adj] {limpio} *tuttzaiuat* [tutïtsaai waht*ï* Wi 126]

close [v] {cerrar} *matzah-tema* [cf. marohtïmarï, close up with hand Wi 43]

close, very [adj] {muy cerca} *icmitz* [cf. miihtsi?, near Wi 45]

cloth [cotton or linen] [n] {lienzo} *tariguanap* [cf. tarïwanap*i*, dry goods, material possessions; wanap*ï*, cloth Wi 146]; (red) cloth {lienzo (colorado)} *ecauanap* [cf. eka-, red color Wi 14; wanap*ï*, cloth Wi 146]

clothing (my) [n] {vestido (mi)} *nenamuiecap* [cf. nï,

my   Wi 67; namahku   Wi 53]

cloud   [n]   {nube}   *tomora-rauet* [cf. tomo-, referring to cloud   Wi 109]

cloudy   [adj]   {nublado}   *to-moahcat* [tomoakatï   Wi 188]

coal   [n]   {carbón}   *cutúbi* [kutuubï   Wi 32]

cobbler   [n]   {zapatero}   *napa-raibo* [cf. napï, shoe   Wi 56; taiboo?, white person   Wi 102]

coffee   [n]   {café}   *tuhpaé,* tu-paé* [cf. huuba?, coffee   Wi 20; tuupï, water (in container, having been brought in)   Wi 126]

coin   [n]   {moneda}   *opés;* copper coin   {moneda de cobre}   *ecauipes* [cf. ekapuhihwi, gold, money, coins   Wi 15]; gold coin   {moneda de oro}   *oauipes* [oha-, prefix referring to yellow color   Wi 71; pu-hihwi, money, gold   Wi 87]; silver coin   {moneda de plata}   *tosauipes* [tosahpuhihwi   Wi 111]

cold [catarrh]   [n]   {catarro}   *onibuecacát* [cf. ohni-ppeh, a cold   Mi 123]

cold   [adj]   {frío}   *etzeit* [ïtsï?-itï   Wi 143]

colt   [n]   {potrillo}   *pucurua* [puku rua?   Wi 88]

comb   [n]   {escarmenador (peine)}   *tzuninatzistuya* [cf. aanatsihtuye?, animal horn comb   Wi 11]

come   [v]   {venir}   *quimaró* [kimarï   Wi 28]

comet   [n]   {cometa}   *tatzinu-pecahpi, tatzinupecabit* [cf. tatsinuupi, star   Wi 105]

compare   [v]   {comparar}   *na-nauchtiuehquitó* [cf. nani?-wiketï, quarrel, argue   Wi 55]

copas (Spanish playing card suit) [n]   {copas (de la baraja)}   *so-coauh* [error: soeoauh; cf. sïï awo, tin cup   Wi 98]

cord or belt to tie the hair, and also otter   [n]   {cordón o cinta para amarrarse los cabellos, y también nutria}   *papi-uehtáma* [papi wïhtama?, otter, mink   Wi 75]

corn [maize]   [n]   {maiz [maíz]}   *janib* [haniibi   Wi 18]

corncob   [n]   {olote}   *janibih-tauorá,* {tusa}   *tetzaya* [hanibitawo?oraa   Wi 18]

corpse   [n]   {muerto (cadáver)}   *teyaep* [tïyaipï   Wi 140]

corral in an arroyo   [n]   {corral en un arroyo}   *junúbi-pucúcane* [cf. hunu?bi, creek Wi 20; puku kahni, pukukïni, stable   Wi 88]

cougar   [n]   {león}   *toyarohco* [toyaruku'   Mc]

cough [n] {tos} *onip* [ohnitï Wi 71]

cover oneself   [v] {taparse} *ejeró* ['ïhïkatï   Wi 142]

coyote [n] {coyote} *tzena* [tseena?   Wi 119]

cramp [n] {calambre} *tzotzone* [cf. tsotsoo?ni, meningitis   Wi 122]

crane [n] {grulla} *nequet* [cf. nïkïta, goose   Wi 67]

crazy [adj] {loco} *poisá* [po?sa   Wi 86]

cricket [n] {grillo} *tuaahtaqui* [cf. tu-, black   Wi 123; aatakíi?, grasshopper   Wi 11]

crook of arm or leg   [n] {corva (la) y también la sangradera (articulación)} *natziminá* [cf. natsimina?, joint   Wi 61]

crooked [adj] {torcido} *onoit* [ono?itï   Wi 72]

cross, Christian   [n] {la cruz} *suabeaep* [suaabe   Wi 95]

cross-eyed [adj] {bizco} *etrapunit* [error: *etzapuinit;** cf. ettsemiH, to close the eyes   Mi 107; wettsepuiH, to blink the eyes   Mi 132]

crow [n] {cuervo} *tujuicá* [tuwikaa?   Wi 126]

crown [top of head]   [n] {mollera} *cueyubó* [cf. ku?e, top Wi 33]

crutch [n] {muleta} *juhpuc* [cf. huu-, wood   Wi 20]

cup, jar, vase   [n] {copa, jarro y vasija} *tei-a-cararaibo*; tin

cup {vaso de hoja de lata} *puyiauh* [cf. puhihwi, money, gold   Wi 87; aawo, cup   Wi 11]

curb [v] {enfrenar} *marepetranicaró*

cut [v] {cortar} *tetziscaró* [tïtsihka?arï   Wi 139]

D

dance [v] {bailar} *nihcaró* [nïhkarï   Wi 67]

dandruff [n] {caspa de la cabeza} *papituhtzaep* [cf. papi, head   Wi 75; tuhtsaipï, dirty object   Wi 124]

darken [v] {oscurecer (el)} *yeinácuere* [cf. ketunabunitï, dark, darken   Wi 28; yeikka, after sundown   Mi 150]

darkness [n] {oscuridad} *quenábunit* [cf. ke-, no   Wi 27; nabunitï, look at oneself Wi 50]

date (of the wild palm)   [n] {dátil (de la palma silvestre)} *mumutziapocope* [cf. mumutsi?, soaproot, yucca   Wi 47; pokopi, fruit   Wi 85], *tabecusé* [cf. tabe-, sun   Wi 99; kusipï, ashes   Wi 32]

daughter-in-law (my)   [n] {nuera (mi)} *nebahpiap* [cf. nï, my   Wi 67; paha piahpï, sister-in-law (of a woman) Wi 74]

dawn [n] {aurora} *nabuni-quit* [cf. tsaa nabuni Wi 113]

day after tomorrow [n] {pasado mañana} *pinacuerena-puetzco* [pi?nakwï bïetsï, pi?naku puetsïku Wi 84]

day before yesterday [n] {anteayer} *equenaquéto* [ek'-ah-nah-kert De94 105]

deaf [adj] {sordo} *quetenacat* [ketïnakatï Wi 28]

deceive [v] {engañar} *nohito* [nohitï Wi 65]

deck of cards [n] {baraja} *guanarohpeté* [cf. wana rohpetirï, play cards Wi 146]

deer [n] {venado} *areca;* Mexican deer {berrendo} *tosarecá* [arïka? Wi 13; tosa-, white, silver Wi 110]

defecate [v] {regir el cuerpo} *cuitaró* [cf. naro?itï, defecate Wi 57; kwiita, buttocks Wi 38]

desire, love [v] {amar, y también querer} *macamaquetó* [cf. kamakïrï Wi 26]

detain [v] {entretener} *nanemucahcacat*

dirt [grime] [n] {mugre (suciedad adherida a la piel)} *tuhtzaep* [tuhtsaipï, dirty object Wi 124]

dirty [adj] {sucio} *tuhtzanoyoit* [cf. nasïseetï, dirty Wi 59; tuhtsaipï, dirty object Wi 124]

do [v] {hacer} *janitó* [cf. hannïtï Wi 18]

doctor [n] {médico} *nafoaiuape* [cf. po'-háh-wi'-e-páh, medicine woman De94 190]

dog [n] {perro} *sarrie* [sarii? Wi 92]

door (movable parts) [n] {puerta (las ojas de la)} *namaréma* [cf. natsahtï, door, doorway Wi 60; namuhyï, doorway Wi 54]

doorway [n] {puerta (el claro de la)} *muyietaet** [moo-hyh-tite De94 85]

double [adj] {doble} *uahnacbac* [cf. waha- Wi 144]

dove [n] {paloma} *cueuó* [ku?e wóo Wi 33]

down [adv] {abajo} *murahcát* [cf. tuhkatï Wi 123]

downpour [n] {lluvia, gota grande} *parahpaet** [cf. pa-, referring to water Wi 73; tapïherï, drop Wi 104]

dream [v] {soñar} *nabusiaep* [nabusi?aipï Wi 50]

dress oneself [v] {vestirse} *namsuaró* [namïsoarï Wi 54]

drink [v] {beber} *jíbito* [hibitï Wi 18]

drizzle [n] {llovizna} *pasibunaet* [pasibunarï, sprinkle (rain) Wi 77]

drop of liquid [n] {gota} *patzohuip* [cf. patso?itï, damp, wet Wi 77]

drum [n] {bombo (tambora)} *sabahpáqui* [cf. pihkarï, drumming Wi 81]; Indian drum {tambor (de los Indios)} *goubiuihtua*

duck [n] {pato} *puêye* [pïïyï Wi 91]

dust [n] {polvo} *júhcup* [huhkupï Wi 20]

E

eagle [n] {águila} *piajuhtzú* [pia huutsuu? Wi 79]

ear [n] {oreja} *náqui* [nakï Wi 52]

earring [n] {arete (zarcillo)} *naquitzáuaco* [cf. nakï tsa?nika? Wi 52]

east [n] {oriente (el)} *muyienaet* [cf. muhyï nakwï Wi 47]

eat [v] {comer} *tehcaró* [tïhkarï Wi 129]

egg (of the birds) [n] {huevo (de las aves)} *nóyo* [nooyo Wi 66]

eight [adj] {ocho} *nameuatzeuhté* [nam'-e-wot-tsooht De94 97]

eighteen [adj] {diez y ocho} *nameuahtzcuhtematoequet* [error: *nameuahtzeuhtematoequet;* nam-e-wot-tsookt-ah-mah-to-y-kut De94 97]

eighteenth [adj] {décimooctavo} *netzasetibitzayacusicuyoje*

eighth [adj] {octavo} *enenaseique*

eighty [adj] {ochenta} *nameuatzeuhtémanri* [cf. nam-i-wat-tsookt-ah-mah-to-y-kut, eighty De94 98]

eighty-one [adj] {ochenta y uno} *nameuatzeuhtenanricemamatoequet* and thus successively repeating the expression meaning "eighty" and that meaning "twelve," "thirteen," etc., up to "nineteen" {y así sucesivamente repitiendo la espresión que significa ochenta y las que significan doce, trece, etc., hasta diez y nueve}[5]

elbow [n] {codo} *quip* [kiipï Wi 28]

eleven [adj] {once} *cemamatoequet* [sim'-áh-máh-to'-y-kut De94 97]

eleventh [adj] {undécimo} *nesuatraicyujé*

entangle [v] {enredar} *mabuecuitzonabó* [cf. kwisiG, to become entangled Mi 116]

enter [v] {entrar} *icaró* [ikarï Wi 23]

equal [v] {igualar} *nanevecaetó* [cf. na?nïbe?, divided evenly Wi 62]

even [adj] {parejo} *seêhpet* [sïïpetï Wi 98]

extend [v] {estender [extender]} *mauchpar*

eye [n] {ojo} *púi* [pui Wi 88]

eyebrow   [n]   {ceja}   *caib*
[ka?ibïï   Wi 26]

eyelash   [n]   {pestaña}   *pursi*
[pot'-see   De94 78]

eyelid   [n]   {párpado}   *puinars*
[pui narïso   Wi 88]

F

fall   [v]   {caer}   *bajitó* [pahitï
Wi 74]

family (my)   [n]   {familia (mi)}
neririeté

fan   [n]   {abanico}   *nehetzauá*
[nïïhïhtsa?wï?   Wi 70]

far   [adj]   {lejos}   *manacuré* [cf.
mana-kkwa   Cr 51]

farmer   [n]   {labrador}   *janibaraibo* [cf. haniibï, corn
Wi 18; paraiboo?, chief Wi 76]

fat   [n]   {sebo}   *oyiuh;*   [adj]
{gordo}   *yuup* [cf. yuhhu,
lard, fat, grease   Wi 158]

father   [n]   {padre}   *ap* [ahpï?
Wi 12]

father-in-law, my   [n]   (man
speaking)   {suegro (del hombre) mi}   *nementóco* [nïmïto-
'ko?   Gl 75]; (woman speaking)   {suegro (de la muger
[mujer]) mi}   *nehutzi-
piap* [cf. nï, my   Wi 67;
hu''cipia'pï? son's wife   Gl
75; ya'hi'pï husband's father
Gl 75]

feather   [n]   {pluma}   *sia* [sie
Wi 93]

female [animal]   [n]   {hembra}
upiab [piabï   Wi 79]

few   [n]   {poco}   *jeihtetzi* [hï-
itïtsi   Wi 22]

fifteen   [adj]   {quince}   *moobetematoequet* [mo'-áh-vit-áh-
máh-to-y-kut   De94 97]

fifteenth   [adj]   {décimoquinto}
netzasenomavinacuyojé

fifth   [adj]   {quinto}
ivinacuyohené

fifty   [adj]   {cincuenta}
moobetémanri

fifty-one   [adj]   {cincuenta
y uno}   *moobetémanri-
cemamatoequet* and successively as explained [below]
with respect to "forty" {y sucesivamente como se esplica
[abajo] respecto a cuarenta}

fight a bull   [v]   {torear}   *cutz-
nanojicuantó* [cf. kuhtsu?,
cow   Wi 30; nohitï, play
Wi 65]

file (tool)   [n]   {lima (instru-
mento)}   *puihgüitzisca* [puiw-
uichtichka, *Feile* (file)   Be
52]

finger   [n]   index finger {dedo
(el índice)}   *tetzitzúca* [tïtsih-
tsuka?   Wi 139]; middle finger {dedo (el mayor o de en
medio)}   *mahtevinat* [mah-
tïpïnaa   Wi 40]; ring finger
{dedo (el anular)}   *mahcatz;*
little finger {dedo (el pequeño
o meñique)}   *mahtua* [mah-
tua?   Wi 40]

fingernail [n] {uña} *masititó* [error: *masihtó;** masiito Wi 44]

fire [n] {lumbre} *cuuna* [cf. kuun*a*, firewood Wi 31]

first [adj] {primero} *namuna-cure* [cf. uk'-er-náhd De94 99]

fish [n] {pescado} *pécui* [painkwi, Mi 126]

fist [n] {puño} *matzocá* [cf. mahtsokaiti, close the hand Wi 40]

five [adj] {cinco} *moobeté* [mo?obe? Wi 46]

flag [n] {bandera} *uanatziá* [wana tsiyaa? Wi 146]; white flag {bandera blanca} *tosanadatziá* [cf. tosa, white Mi 142; wana tsiyaa? Wi 146]

flank [n] {lomo} *ojótoco* [ohutuki, flank of animal Wi 71; cf. **back**]

flat-nosed [adj] {chato (el de nariz aplastada)} *muviyeh-pap* [cf. muhbi, nose Wi 47]

flatulence [n] {ventosidad} *pisup* [cf. pisi'uh, to break wind Mi 130]

flea [n] {pulga} *ecapusia* [ekapusi?*a* Wi 15]

flint [n] {piedra de lumbre} *tetecae* [narak, *Feuerstein* (flint) Be 53]

flower [n] {la flor en general} *sahtotzip** [cf. totsiyaapi, flower Wi 111; saatotsiya,

flowering plant Wi 91]; **flower** (of the wild palm) {flor (de la palma silvestre)} *sahtotziyiap* [cf. saatotsiya, flowering plant Wi 91]

fly [insect] [n] {mosca} *ani-mui* [animu*i* Wi 12]

foam of water [n] {espuma del agua} *sahtotzip* [cf. saahto-tsito?i? Wi 91]; foam or spittle of a horse {espuma o baba del caballo} *sohcap* [cf. yo-kapi, phlegm, juice Wi 158]

fold [n] {doblez} *sómaet* [cf. masomiH, to fold Mi 117]

foot [n] {pie} *napé* [naap*e* Wi 49]

forehead [n] {frente} *caé* [ka?i Wi 26]

forty [adj] {cuarenta} *ayaro-cuetémanri* [cf. hi'-yáh-ro-quet-sa'-im-en De94 97]

forty-one [adj] {cuarenta y uno} *ayarocuetémanri-cemamatoequet* and thus successively repeating the expression meaning "forty" and that meaning "twelve," "thirteen," etc., up to "nineteen" {y así sucesivamente repitiendo la espresion [expresión] que significa cuarenta y las que significan doce, trece, etc., hasta diez y nueve}[6]

four [adj] {cuatro} *ayarocueté* [hayarokweti Wi 18]

fourteen [adj] {catorce} *aya-rocuetemantoéquet* [hi'-yáh-

ro-quet-áh-máh-to'-y-kut
De94 97]

fourteenth [adj] {décimocuarto}
netzaseinonaiá

fourth [adj] {cuarto} *enesuativinacuere*

frightened [to be frightened] [v]
{asustarse y espantarse}
omacuiyaró [cf. kuya?arï
Wi 33]

frog [n] {rama [rana]} *pasauiyió* [pos-so-we'-yo
De94 124]

from ahead [adv] {por de-
lante} *nemunácuere* [cf.
munakwï, ahead Wi 179]

from behind [adv] {por de-
trás} *nevinácuere* [cf. pi-
nakwï, behind Wi 182]

frost [n] {helada} *tosanebaep*
[tosa nïïbaai? Wi 111] *tosa-
nebaehcat* [tosa nïïbaikatï
Wi 111]

fruit (of any tree or plant) [n]
{fruto (de cualquier árbol o
planta)} *pocope* [pokop*i*
Wi 85]

G

gall [n] {hiel} *upúi, opúi**
[pu?i? gall bladder Wi 89]

garbage (leftovers) [n] {basura
(sobras de la comida)} *te-
queuéhtlap* [error: *tequeuehtiap;** cf. tïkï toip*i*, leftover
food Wi 131]

give [v] {dar} *nautoró* [cf.
na-, reflexive prefix Wi 49;
uttuH, give Mi 146]

glass [drinking glass] [n]
{vaso} *aguó* [aawo Wi 11;
cf. paboko aawo Wi 73]

glue [n] {pegadura (cola o al-
midón)} *chaco;* [v] {pegar
(unir una cosa con pegadura a
otra)} *chahpaquitó*

go [v] {ir} *miar* [miarï Wi
45]; go down {bajar} *ueto*

goat [n] {ganado cabrío}
chiva [cf. sippeh, sheep
Mi 134]

God [n] {Dios} *taahpue* [Ta?-
ahpï, Our Father, Great Spirit
Wi 105], *tatoco* [cf. tahï, our
Wi 102; toko?, maternal
grandfather Wi 109]

gold [n] {oro} *oaui* [cf. oha-,
prefix referring to yellow
color Wi 71; puhihwi,
money, gold Wi 87]

gold coins (Spanish playing card
suit) [n] {oros (los de la baraja)} *ojapite* [cf. oha-, prefix
referring to yellow color Wi
71; puhihwi, money, gold
Wi 87]

good [adj] {bueno} *tzat*
[tsaatï Wi 113]

gourd [n] {guaje} *oteauh*
[cf. ottsa, jug Mi 124; aawo,
cup Wi 11]

grandchild (my) [n] {nieto y
neita (mi)} *netoco* or *neroco*
[cf. nï, my Wi 67; toko?,

man's uterine grandchild   Wi
109]

grandfather   [n] {abuelo} *róco*
[toko?, maternal grandfather
Wi 109]; grandfather (my)
{abuelo (mi)} *neroco* or *netoco* [cf. nï, my   Wi 67]

grandmother   [n] {abuela}
cáco [kaku?   Wi 26]; grandmother (my)   {abuela (mi)}
necoco [cf. nï, my   Wi 67]

grandson (grandmother speaking)   [n] {nieto (respecto a la
abuela)}   *tutzi* [cf. hu''ci?
Gl 74]

grape   [n] {uva}   *natramuese*
[error: *natzamucoe;* natsa-
mukwe?   Wi 60]

grass   [n] {zacate}   *sonip*
[sonipï   Wi 94]

grasshopper (locust)   [n] {cha-
pulín (langosta)}   *aahtaqui*
[aatakii?   Wi 11]

gray hair   [n] {cana}   *uétzi*
[cf. esi-, gray   Wi 16]

great-grandchildren (my)   [n]
{biznietos (mis)}   *nequenotzine* [cf. nï, my   Wi 67;
kenu, grandchild   Mi 112]

grind [crush]   [v] {moler}   *tetzocuetó* [tatsukwerï, mash,
crush, smash   Wi 105]

guards   [n] {guardas}
tarenamó*

gullet   [n] {esófago}   *ucútz*
[cf. kuitsï, throat   Wi 30]*

gum   [n] {goma}   *sanahpi*

[sana"-pin, pitch, sap of a tree
Mi 133], *uoniayaquep* [cf.
owóora, tree trunk   Wi 73;
yokapï, phlegm, juice   Wi
158]; chewing gum   [n]
{chitle [chicle]}   *sanahco* [cf.
sanahkoo? kïtsïkwetï   Wi
91]

gums   [n] {encías}   *tamaruhc*
[cf. taama, tooth   Wi 99;
tuhku, flesh   Wi 123]

gunpowder   [n] {pólvora}
nacútusí, nacutzi [nakutïsi
Wi 52]

H

hackberry (tree)   [n] {palo-
blanco (planta)}   *querajú*
[kïrahuu?   Wi 35]

hail   [n] {granizo}   *pahopi* [pa-
hoopi   Wi 74]

hair   [n] {bello [pelo] (en general)}   *puêjep* [piáhp   De94
78]; hair of the head {cabello}
papi [papi, head   Wi 75];
pubic hair   {bello (el del em-
peine)}   *súji* [cf. tso?yaa?,
head of hair, hair   Wi 122];
underarm hair   {bello (de la
arca)}   *amáfe* [cf. ama, waist
Mi 106; ahna, underarm
Wi 11]

half   [n] {mitad (la)}
matocuehtevinauequico

halter or lariat   [n] {cabestro o

reata} *uiyá* [cf. pahki wiyaa?,
rope of rawhide Wi 74]

hand [n] {mano} *moo* [mo?o
Wi 46]

hand over [v] {entregar}
caneaequicuató

hang [v] {colgar} *negünitó*
[nïïkwenitï, hang oneself
Wi 70]

happy [adj] {feliz} *quehenanesuaet* [cf. tsaa nïïsukatï
Wi 113]

hardly [adv] {apenas} *jimatác*
[himataaka, barely Wi 18]

hare [n] {liebre} *piarabo*
[cf. piaravukina:', jack-
rabbit Mc]

hat [n] {sombrero} *suparello,* supareyos, uihtuabape*
[cf. wittua, pot, pan, cup
Cr 98; pap*i*, head Wi 75]

haul [v] {cargar} *noró* [noorï,
haul away Wi 66]

headache [n] {dolor de ca-
beza} *papicamacat* [cf.
pap*i*kamaka natïsu?u, aspirin
(lit. "headache medicine")
Wi 75]

headboard of bed [n] {cabe-
cera} *uequitzóhpe* [cf. tsohp*e*,
pillow Wi 121]

headstall [n] {jáquima} *necobetzanica* [cf. nakobe
tsa?nika?, halter Wi 52]

hear [v] {oir} *tenacaró* [tïna-
karï, hear something Wi
134]

hearing [n] {oído (el)} *naquitaet* [cf. nakarï, hear Wi 52]

heart [n] {corazón} *opíh*
[pih*i* Wi 170]

heat [n] {calor} *ereit* [ïrï?itï,
hot weather Wi 143]

heel [n] {talón} *tahpicó*
[tahp*i*ko?, heel of shoe
Wi 101; tap*i*ko?, heel of
foot Wi 104]

here [adv] {aquí} *iquite*
[cf. ik*i* Wi 23]

heron [n] {garza} *cusihcuá*
and *tunequi* [kusikwa?aa?
Wi 31; cf. tu-, black, dark
Wi 123; nïkïta goose Wi 67]

hers [adj, pron] {su, suyo} *ma*
[ma, him, her, it Wi 39]

hiccup [n] {hipo} *jéni* [hï?-
niip*i*? Wi 23]*

hide oneself [v] {esconderse}
uatzavitó [wats*i* habiitï
Wi 147]

high [adj] {alto} *pagüenér* [cf.
pa?atï Wi 78]

hill [n] {cerro} *toyábi* [toya,
toyaab*i*, mountain Wi 112];
little hill {cerro pequeño}
tiehtoyábi [tïe little Wi 128]

his [adj, pron] {su, suyo} *ma*
[ma, him, her, it Wi 39]

hoe [n] {azadón} *cujorá*
[kuw*i*hora? Wi 32]

hold fast [n] {tener} *tequiheató* [cf. kwïhïrï, arrest, capture, catch Wi 39]

hole [n] {agujero} *taet* [taaitï

Wi 99]; hole (in ear for earring) {agujero (de la oreja
para el arete)} *naquitárauet*
[nak*i*, ear   Wi 52]

honey   [n] {miel} *uobipihuab*
[cf. wobi, ref. to wood   Wi
149; cf. wobi p*i*hnaa?   Wi
149]

horn [of animal]   [n] {cuerno}
oá   [aa   Wi 11]

horse   [n] {caballo} *puc*
[puuk*u*, puki   Wi 88], *tehi*
[error: *tehei;** t*i*h*i*ya   Wi
129]; mustang {caballo me-
steño} *cóbe* [cf. Kobi, Wild
Horse (person's name)   Ma
406; kobi, *Hengst* (stallion)
Be 52]

horsefly   [n] {tábano} *pihpitz*
[pihp*i*   Wi 81]

hot   [adj] {caliente} *ereit*
[*i*r*i*?it*i*, hot weather   Wi 143]

house   [n] {casa} *caane* [error:
caani;* kahni   Wi 24]

hummingbird   [n] {colibrí o
chupa-rosa} *temumuquit*

hungry   [adj] {hambriento}
tziareyiajumiar [cf. tsihasu-
ar*i*   Wi 120]

hurricane   [n] {huracán}
quehtanet [k*i*htáan*i*et*i*, storm,
blow hard   Wi 34]

husband   [n] {marido} *cumahpue* [kumahp*i*?   Wi 201]

hush   [v] {callar} *subecatecua*
[cf. sube?su, immediately
Wi 96; ke-, no   Wi 27; tek-
war*i*, speak   Wi 107]

I

I   [pron] {yo} *ne* [n*i*?   Wi 70]

ice   [n] {hielo} *uehpahcaecat*
[cf. pakka-ppyh, ice, glass
Cr 66]

intestine   [n] {tripa} *ucuitatz*
[kwitats*i*, "large intestine"
Wi 38]

iron   [n] {hierro} *puihgüi* [cf.
puhihwi, money or gold
Wi 87]

its   [adj, pron] {su, suyo} *ma*
[ma, him, her, it   Wi 39]

J

jack (playing card)   [n] {sota
(de la baraja)} *taibo* [taiboo?,
white person   Wi 102]

jaguar   [n] {tigre} *naboróyarohco* [cf. naboohroya
ruhku?, leopard   Wi 50]

jar, cup, vase   [n] {copa, jarro y
vasija} *tei-a-caraibo*

javelina   [n] {javalí} *sapayé*
[cf. wasape'a, bear   Mc]

jeer   [n] {burla, mofe [mofa]*}
tenisuyaet [cf. t*i*n*i*usu?uyait*i*,
jeer at   Wi 134]

jerky   [n] {cecina} *inap* [inap*i*
Wi 23]; pieces of jerky {tasa-
jos (de carne seca)} *uehtuné*

join   [v] {juntar} *tzómeto*
[tso?meet*i*, gather   Wi 122]

joint [inside of elbow or knee]
[n] {sangradera y también la

corva} *natziminá* [natsimina? Wi 61]

jug [n] {jarro} *socoauó* [error: *soeoauó*; cf. soo, much   Wi 94; aawo, cup   Wi 11]

jump [v] {brincar y saltar} *pohpitó* [pohpï tï   Wi 84]

K

kill [v] {matar} *pehcaró* [pehkarï   Wi 79]

king (playing card) [n] {rey (de la baraja)} *taibouiahpe* [cf. taiboo?, white person   Wi 102; wa'ippe, woman   Mi 146]

kiss [n] {beso (sustantivo)} *murraé* [cf. muhrarï, kiss someone   Wi 47]

kite [bird] [n] {milano} *auequebrahcuasi*

knee [n] {rodilla} *tandap* [tana, tanapï   Wi 104]

knife [n] {cuchillo} *uí* [wiiyu, awl, ice pick   Wi 149]

knoll [n] {loma} *anábi* [anabi, one hill   Wi 12]

know [of or about] [v] {conocer y saber} *osupanaet* [cf. supana?itï, knowing   Wi 96]

L

lame [adj] {cojo} *uinaét* [wihnaitï, crippled   Wi 148]

lance [n] {lanza} *tzie* [tïtsiwaii?   Wi 139]

land [n] {tierra} *socobí* [sokoobï   Wi 94]

lariat or halter [n] {cabestro o reata} *uiyá* [pahki wiyaa?, rope of rawhide   Wi 74]

laugh [n] {risa} *yahnet*; laugh at [v] {reirse} *yahneto* [cf. yahneetï, (v) laugh   Wi 157]

lead [metal] [n] {plomo} *nabacaet* [cf. nabaaka, bullet   Wi 49]

leaf (of ear of corn) [n] {hoja (de la mazorca del maíz)} *janibitapuip* [cf. hani buhipï   Wi 18]

leather [n] {cuerno [error: cuero*]} *taibobicap* [taibo pikapï, leather (commercially prepared; lit. "white man leather")   Wi 102]

leave [v] {salir} *junacoroito* [cf. hunakïhu, toward the outside   Wi 20]

leech [n] {sanguijuela} *tuure* [tu?re?   Wi 126]

left [side, direction] [n] {lado izquierdo, la izquierda} *neoihninácure* [cf. nï, my   Wi 67; ohinikatï, left-handed   Wi 71]

leg [n] {pierna (la)} *omo* [oomo, lower leg   Wi 72]

liar [n] {embustero, mentiroso} *isap* [isapï   Wi 23]

lie down [v] {acostarse} *jabitó* [habiitï   Wi 17]

light [n] {luz} *tzanábubit* [cf.
tsaa, good   Wi 112; nabun-
itï, look at oneself   Wi 50];
artificial light {luz artificial}
ecacusayet [cf. ekakwitse?e,
lightening flash   Wi 14]

lightning [n] {relámpago}
ecahcuitzet [ekakwitse?e,
lightning flash   Wi 14]

limp [v] {cojer [cojear]}
yocoró [cf. yïkarï, walk
Wi 159]

lip (lower)   [n] {labio (el inferior)} *tuhcanancurehtep* [to'-
káhn-ok-wu-tip'   De94 78];
lip (upper) {labio (el superior)} *panacuerehtep* [pan'-
ok-wa-tip'   De94 78]

liver [n] {hígado} *onem* [cf.
nïïmï   Wi 70]

locust (grasshopper)   [n] {cha-
pulín (langosta)} *aahtaqui*
[aatakii?, grasshopper   Wi
11]

look [v] {mirar} *bunitó*
[punitï   Wi 88]

loose [adj] {flojo} *tiohnab*

loosen [v] {soltar} *mavuearó*

louse [n] {piojo} *pusia*
[pusi?a   Wi 88]

love, desire [v] {amar, y también querer} *macamaquetó*
[cf. kamakïrï   Wi 26]

lung [n] {pulmón, el bofe*}
osom, osomo* [cf. soomo
Wi 95]

M

maguey [n] {maguey} *muranáqui* [cf. muura?, mule
Wi 48; naki, ear   Wi 52];
maguey stalk and also bulrush
{tule y también quiote} *pamoc* [error: *pamoe*; cf.
pamu, watercress   Mi 124;
pa?mutsi, plant similar to
water lily   Wi 78]

male [n] {macho} *ucuma*
[cf. kuhma   Wi 30]

man [n] {hombre} *tenahpua*
[tenahpï?   Wi 107]; old man
{anciano} *chucuhpua* [cf.
sukuupï   Wi 96]

mane [n] {crin} *oania* [ania
Wi 12]; horse's mane* {crin
de caballo} *tejeiania* [tïhïya
ania   Wi 12]

marrow [n] {tuétano} *otuh*
[cf. otï-, brown   Wi 72]

mask [n] {jáquima} *nacobetzanica* [cf. kobe tsa?nika?
Wi 28]

meal [n] {comida} *narehcá*
[cf. tïkï, ref. to food   Wi
130]

meat [n] {carne} *tehcap* [tïh-
kapa   Wi 129]

melon [n] {melón} *taibobinap*
[cf. taibo bihnaa?, canta-
loupe   Wi 102]

mesquite [n] {mesquite}
uohné [error: *uohué*;*
wohihu   Wi 149]

Mexican, or white man   [n]
{gente, o Mexicano} *tabebo,
taibo, araibo** [cf. taiboo?,
non-Indian, white person
Wi 102; yuu taibo?, Mexican,
lit. "fat white man"   Wi 159]

midnight   [n] {media noche}
tocuehtucan [tokwetukan
Wi 109]

milk   [n] {leche} *petzip* [error:
*pitzip;** pitsipɨ   Wi 83]

Milky Way   [n] {Via lactea}
esiavit [cf. Esihabiitɨ, Gray-
streak (person's name)   Wi
16]

mirror   [n] {espejo} *naboné*
[nabuni?   Wi 50]

mockingbird   [n] {cenzontle}
soyáque [soo yake?   Wi 95]

molar   [n] {muela (diente molar)} *piarama;* molars {mue-
las (dientes molares)} *piviarama* [cf. pia, large   Wi 79;
taama, tooth   Wi 99]

mole [animal]   [n] {topo}
cuminé [kumi'ne'   Mc]

moon   [n] {luna} *muea* [mɨa
Wi 48]

morning   [n] {mañana (la)}
puetzconacuere [cf.
pɨetsɨku   Wi 89]

morning star   [n] {estrella de la
mañana (Vénus)} *tahtatzi-
nupi* [tah'-tats-ee-nap   De94
133]

mosquito   [n] {mosco} *muchicua* [mutsikwà?aa?   Wi

48]; {mosquito} *tiremuchicua* [cf. tɨe, little   Wi 128;
mutsikwà?aa?, mosquito
Wi 48]

mother   [n] {madre} *pia* [pia
Wi 79]; mother (my) {madre
(mi)} *nevia* [cf. nɨ, my   Wi
67; pia, mother   Wi 79]

mother-in-law, my   [n] (man
speaking) {suegra (del hombre) mi} *nemencaco* [nɨmɨka-
'ku?   Gl 74]; (woman speaking) {suegra (de la muger,
[mujer]) mi} *neyahipue* [cf.
nɨ, my   Wi 67; ya'hi'pɨ?, husband's mother   Gl 75]

mount   [v] {subir} *toito* [cf.
to'ih, to climb   Mi 141;
tɨhɨya ro?itɨ, climb on horseback   Wi 130]

mouth   [n] {boca} *tep* [tɨɨpe
Wi 140]

much   [adj] {mucho} *jéyiu,
sote* [soo   Wi 94]

mucus   [n] {mocos} *muuisip*
[error: *muvisip;** mupisippeh,
snot   Mi 119]

mulberry (tree)   [n] {mora (árbol)} *sohobocopi* [soho
bo?koo? huupi   Wi 165];
fruit {mora (fruta)} *eteaé* [cf.
etehupʔ, red mulberry tree
CJ 523; etɨhuupi, osage or-
ange tree   Wi 16]

musician   [n] {músico} *goineroibo* [cf. piawoin, *Trompete*
(trumpet)   Be 53; Pi-ha-gwai-

na, The drummer (*sic,* Washakie's name) Fo 269; taiboo?, white man Wi 102]

mustang [n] {caballo mes-
teño} *cóbe* [cf. Kobi, Wild
Horse (person's name) Ma
406; kobi, *Hengst* (stallion)
Be 52]

mute [person] [n] {mudo}
quetécuahcat [cf. ketekwa,
dumb Wi 27]

my [adj] {mío} *nea* [cf. nï
(first-person exclusive genitive
singular pronoun), my Wi
67; cf. nïe (first-person accusative singular pronoun), me
Wi 67]

N

narrow [adj] {angosto} *tieuegquité;* very narrow {ango-
stito} *tieuehquitetzi* [cf. ty-
waikkih-tyn, ty-wekkih-tyn
Cr 156]

navel [n] {ombligo} *osíco* [cf.
siikï̈ Wi 93]

near [adv] {cerca (adverbio)}
mihtetzi [miitïtsi Wi 45]

neck [n] {pescuezo} *toyop*
[toyopï̈ Wi 112]

necklace [n] {collar} *córohc*
[kotokki Cr 43]

needle [n] {aguja} *uanatzahquená* [wana tsahkïna? Wi
146]

Negro [n] {Negro (el afri-

cano)} *tuhpísi* [cf. tuu-
ppysaah, dark Cr 111; tuht-
aiboo?, black person Wi 124]

nephew (my) [n] {sobrino
(mi)} *neruce,* the same as **son**
[error: *nerua;* nï, my Wi 67;
tua?, son Wi 123]

nerve [n] {nervio} *támo* [cf.
tammu, cord, sinew Mi
136]

nest [n] {nido} *juhtzu a caané*
[huutzu?a kahni Wi 21]

new [adj] {nueve [nuevo]}
equebitz [cf. ïkï, recently, ïkï-,
young Wi 142; -pittseh,
noun suffix Mi 20]

niece (my) [n] {sobrina (mi)}
nerete [cf. nï, my Wi 67;
ara?, man's sister's child
Wi 13]

night [n] {noche} *tucan* [tu-
kaani Wi 124]

nine [adj] {nueve} *cemanouehminate* [cf. wo'-me-nut
De94 97]

nineteen [adj] {diez y nueve}
cemanoueminatematoequet

nineteenth [adj] {décimonono}
netzaribitzayacusicuyoje

ninety [adj] {noventa} *ce-
manouchminatemanri* [error:
cemanouehminatemanri*] [cf.
sim'-ah-wo'-me-nut De94
98]

ninety-one [adj] {noventa y
uno} *cemanouchminateman-
ricemamatoequet* [error:
cemanouehminatemanrice-

mamatoequet*] and thus successively repeating the expression meaning "ninety" and that meaning "eleven," "twelve," "thirteen," etc., up to "nineteen" {y así sucesivamente repitiendo la espresión que significa noventa y las que significan once, doce, trece, etc., hasta diez y nueve}[7]

ninth [adj] {noveno} *netzaicyujé*

nit [n] {liendre} *pusiárachi* [cf. pus*i*?a, head louse   Wi 88]

no [adv] {no} *tocusé, niatz** [neatz, *nein* (no)   Be 53]

noon [n] {medio día} *tocuehtaben* [tokwetabeni   Wi 109]

north [n] {norte (el)} *cuihné* [cf. kwihnenakw*ï*   Wi 38]

North Star [n] {estrella del Norte} *tatzinupi-puetuhcatutamiae* [tatsinuup*i*, star   Wi 105]

nose [n] {nariz} *muvi* [mubi Wi 47]; aquiline nose {nariz aguileña} *murauar;* turned-up nose {nariz arremangada} *muitar*

nostril [n] {ventana (de la nariz)} *muvitaet* [cf. mubi, nose   Wi 47; taait*ï*, hole Wi 99; nemobitain, *Nasenlöcher* (nostril)   Be 51]

nothing [n] {nada} *quehetza* [cf. kehena   Wi 27]

now [adv] {ahora} *equihtzí* [kihitsi?   Wi 28]

O

oak, evergreen [n] {chaparro prieto, planta} *tujuhpi* [tuhuupi, tuhu huupi, blackjack oak   Wi 124]

offspring [n] {parto (el)} *guaihputzarua* [cf. wa'ippe, woman   Mi 146; tua?, son Wi 123]

[ogre] Imaginary being that they suppose is in human form, gigantic, that carries an extraordinarily large staff of wood, that eats men, that lives in some large caves that are in some mountains very far to the north; they believe that when he breaks the staff, they die   [n] {Ser imaginario que suponen es de figura humana, gigantesco, que porta como bastón un palo estraordinariamente grande, que se come a los hombres, que habita en unas cerros al Norte, muy lejos. Creen que cuando se le rompe el bastón se muere.} *piamupitz* [cf. pia, big Wi 80; mom-pittseh, owl Mi 118; mupits*i*, giant   Wi 48]

old [adj] {viejo (adjetivo)} *puetep* [cf. p*ï*et*ï*p*ï*, elderly woman   Wi 89]

one [adj] {uno} *cíen* [cf. sïmï Wi 97]

open [v] {abrir} *matzitjuaró*

otter and also cord or belt to tie the hair [n] {nutria, y también el cordón o cinta con que se amarran los cabellos} *papiuehtama* [pap*i* wïhtama? Wi 75]

outfit, feather [n] {trage de pluma} *senoé*

owe something [v] {deber algo} *sucuitae*

owl [n] {tecolote} *mupitz, neminoet* [mom-pittseh Mi 118] screech or barn owl {lechuza} *ooa* [o?oo Wi 73]

P

pain in arm [n] {dolor en el brazo} *puerahcamacat* [cf. pïïr*a*, arm Wi 91; kammah-kantyn, to have pain Cr 40]; pain in legs {dolor de piernas} *omocamacat* [cf. omo-, oomo, lower leg Wi 72; kammah-kantyn, to have pain Cr 40]

paint [v] {pintar} *tebor* [cf. tïboorï, write Wi 128]

painter [n] {pintor} *teboet* [cf. tïboorï, write Wi 128]

palm (of hand) [n] {palma (de la mano)} *mahpána* [mapaan*a* Wi 43]; palm (plant)

{palma (planta)} *mumutzi* [mumutsi?, yucca Wi 47]

pants [n] {pantalones} *cus* [kusa Mi 114]

paper [n] {papel} *temacuatui* [cf. tïmakwatui?, cigarette wrapper plant Wi 132]

[parfleche] cover of anything closed with leather straps [n] {cubierta de cualquiera cosa cerrada con correas} *oyoté* [oyoote? Wi 73]

partridge [n] {codorniz} *tirehbasu* [tïrïe basuu, quail Wi 137]

peach [n] {durazno} *piviaronab* [cf. pia, big Wi 79; tuhnaséka Mexican persimmon Wi 123]

pecan [n] {nuez (la encarcelada)} *naquehtábae* [nakkï-taba?i Wi 52]

pelt [probably used as a saddlecloth] [n] {pelon [pellón]} *osacurauoar* [cf. tsahk-wïrïarï (v), skin animal Wi 114]

penis [n] {pene} *güêa* [wean Mi 147]

persimmon tree [n] {níspero} *naséca* [naseka Wi 59]

petticoat [n] {enaguas} *pínica*

phlegm [n] {baba} *sóhcap* [cf. yokap*i* Wi 158]

pig [n] {marrano (cerdo)} *muviporo* [mub*i* po?roo? Wi 46]

pillow [n] {almohada} *tzóhpe* [tsohpe Wi 121]

pinole [flour from ground mesquite beans] [n] {pinole} *pinarusup* [cf. pihnaa?, sugar Wi 81]

pipe for smoking [n] {pipa para fumar} *tói* [to?i Wi 112]

pistol, six-shooter [n] {pistola de seis tiros} *natzahcuinó* [natsahkwine? Wi 60]

play [v] {jugar} *nojitó* [nohitï Wi 65]

Pleiades [n] {Pléyadas (las siete cabrillas)} *sóte*

plowman [n] {arador} *tetzóteuei* [cf. tïtsa?woo?, plow; tïtsa?worï, plow soil Wi 139]

plum [n] {tejocote} *amauó* [cf. amawoo, apple Wi 12; sïkï?i, plum Wi 97]

pocketknife [n] {navaja} *jábi*

poncho (fine) [n] {jorongo (fino)} *patzinacusi* [cf. pattsi, smooth, shiny Mi 128; kwasu?u, coat Wi 37]; (ordinary) poncho {jorongo (ordinario)} *eh* [ehe, blanket, shawl Mi 107]

poor [adj] {pobre} *tetanahcat*

porcupine [n] {erizo (quadrúpedo)} *junáu* [hïïnï? Wi 22]

pot, small [n] {ollita} *nehotzqitaen**

potato [n] {papa} *toroponí*

[cf. to?roponii?, beetlike tuber Wi 112]

prickly pear fruit [n] {tuna} *ocuebocopi* [cf. wokwéesi, prickly pear cactus Wi 150; pokopi, fruit Wi 85]

promise [v] {prometer} *janiquetó*

pumpkin [n] {calabaza} *nacusí* [nakwïsi Wi 53]

pus [n] {podre} *pisip* [pisi Wi 82]

Q

quadruple [adj] {cuádruple} *ayarocuetenacbaco* [cf. hi'-yàh-ro-quet, four De94 97]

quarrel [v] {pelear} *navitequetó* [cf. nani?wiketï Wi 55]

quintuple [adj] {quíntuple} *movetenacbaco* [mo'-àh-vit, five De94 97]

quirt [n] {cuarta (chicote)} *pucugüehpaé* [cf. puku, horse Wi 88; wïapa?arï, beat up Wi 151]

quiver [n] {carcax} *jucuni* [hoo'-koon-àh De94 88]

R

rabbit [n] {conejo} *tábo* [cf. tabu?kina? Wi 100]

rain, shower [n] {aguacero y también lluvia} *emar* [ïmaarï Wi 143]

rainbow [n] {arco-iris} *para-coa* [cf. pa-, ref. to water, Wi 73; tokoa, snake Mi 141; pisi ma?rokóo? Wi 82]

rainspell [n] {temporal de agua} *paêmá* [paa'ema, to rain Mi 124]

ram [n] {carnero} *cuajaré* [cf. kwahaten, antelope Mi 115]

rat [n] {ratón} *caa* [cf. kaan Mi 167]

rattle of snake [n] {cascabel de víbora} *uehquétzutzu* [cf. wïhkitsu?tsuki? Wi 151]

ray of light [n] {ecshalación [exhalación]} *tatzinupi-bajin* [cf. tatsinuupi, star Wi 105]

reed [n] {carrizo} *jucáhpi;* bulrush, maguey stalk {tule y también quiote} *pamoc* [er-ror: *pamoe;* cf. pamu, water-cress Mi 124; pa?mutsi, plant similar to water lily Wi 78]

rejoice [v] {alegrarse} *naoquit* [na?okitï, Wi 62]

return [v] {volver} *coehquí* [koihki Mi 113]

rib [n] {costilla} *oguáhtze* [cf. kwahtsï Wi 37]

rich [adj] {rico} *tzanahcat* [tsaa naahkatï Wi 113]

rifle, carbine [n] {carabina, y también fusil} *piaet* [cf. pia, big Wi 79; eetï, bow Wi 14; piai, *Gehehr* (*Feuer-*) (rifle) Be 53]

right side, direction [n] {lado derecho, la derecha} *nerivitzinacure*

ring [n] {anillo (tumbaga)} *motzinica* [mo?o tsi?nika? Wi 46]

Rio Grande [n] {Río-Bravo} *ocuebi* [cf. okweetu, stream Wi 72; Kwana kuhtsu paa?, Rio Grande Wi 37]

rise [v] {levantar} *yetzeró* [yïtsïrï, rise up, go up, fly up Wi 160]

river [n] {río}, large arroyo {arroyo grande} *piajunubi* [pia, big Wi 79; hunu?bi, stream Wi 20]

road [n] {camino} *pué* [pu?e Wi 89]

roadrunner [n] {corre-camino} *ebicuyonit* [cf. eebi, blue Wi 14; kuyu?nii, turkey Wi 33]

rob [v] {quitar con corage} *eyacraitoihné* [cf. jaa', take Cr 36]

robe [n] {túnico} *pihiboa* [cf. pïpï?, hair fuzz, animal hide, sheep wool, hairy vegetation Wi 90]

roof [n] {techo} *namarema* [cf. namuhyï, door Wi 60]

rooster [n] {gallo} *tayáque* [cf. taa-, ref to morning Wi 99; yaketï, cry, make noise Wi 157]

rope [v] {lazar} *teconicaquetó*
roughness [n] {escabrosidad}
uohtzaut
rude [adj] {malcriado, gro-
sero} *quesuat* [cf. ke-, no
Wi 27; suarï, thought Wi
95]
run [v] {correr} *nuhquitó*
[nuhkitï Wi 66]

S

sadden [to be saddened] [v]
{entristecerse} *tetanasuat* [cf.
tetteha, to be sad Mi 140;
na-, reflexive prefix Wi 48;
suatïtï, think Wi 96]
saddle [n] {silla (de montar)}
narenó [narino, *Sattel*
(saddle) Be 53; narïnoo?,
pack saddle Wi 58]; [v]
{ensillar} *nerenorequitó*
[narïnoo?rïkitï, saddle up
Wi 58]
saddlebag [n] {maleta} *pigusoa* [piksorh, *Satteltasche*
(saddlebag) Be 53]
saddle pad [n] {grupera}
noctzitzanica [error: *noetzitzanica;** cf. natsanïhkï?,
saddle girth Wi 60]
sailboat [n] {buque de vela}
parumíaet [cf. pa-, ref. to
water Wi 73; miarï, go
Wi 45]
saliva [n] {saliva} *tusip*
[tusipï Wi 125]

salt [n] {sal} *onabi* [onaabi
Wi 72]
saltpeter [n] {salitre o sal-
tierra} *ona* [cf. ona-, ref.
to salt Wi 72]
sand [n] {arenilla} *pasinape*
[error: *pasiuape*; cf. pasi
waapi Wi 77]; lacrimal sand
{laganas} *pisibui* [cf. pisi, pus
Wi 82; pui, eye Wi 88]
saw [n] {sierra (de carpintero)}
juhtziscá [huutsihkaa?, two-
man handsaw Wi 21]
scab [n] {caspa} *tuhtzaep*
[cf. tuhtsaipï, dirty object
Wi 124]
scalp [n] {piel (de la cabeza)}
tzohpoá {cf. tso?yaa?, hair
Wi 122; po?a, skin Wi 85]
scapula [n] {paleta (de la es-
palda)} *usihcop* [cf. seehk'-
kope, shoulder blade De94 79]
scatter [v] {sembrar} *tetzabor*
[cf. tsahperï Wi 114]
scissors [n] {tijeras} *néhtzisque* [nechziske, *Scheere* (sic,
scissors) Be 52; cf. wana
koo?, Wi 146]
sea [n] {mar} *tibitzi-piacuebi*
[cf. tepitsi, very Mi 140; tïbitsi, really, surely Wi 127;
pia, big Wi 79; okweetï,
stream Wi 72]
second [adj] {segundo} *mavinacure* [cf. o'-ve-nok De94
99]
sell [v] {vender} *temuer* [cf.
temeeH, to buy Mi 139]

send [v] {mandar y también remitir} *maritanahcat*

seven [adj] {siete} *tatzeuhté* [cf. tàh'-tsookt De94 97]

seventeen [adj] {diez y siete} *tatzeutematoequet* [tàh'-tsookt-àh-màh-to'-y-kut De94 97]

seventeenth [adj] {décimosétimo} *netzaseayacuasicyojé*

seventh [adj] {séptimo} *enenaseiqueuên*

seventy [adj] {setenta} *totzeuhtemanri* [cf. tàh'-tsookt-sa'-im-in De94 98]

seventy-one [adj] {setenta y uno} *totzeuhtemanri-cemamatoequet* and thus successively, as explained [below] for "sixty[-two]" {y así sucesivamente, como se ha dicho respecto a sesenta}

sew [v] {coser} *tetzasquenaró* [tïtsahkïnarï Wi 138]

shadow [n] {sombra} *jequiacat* [cf. hïhkiapï Wi 22]

shame [n] {vergüenza} *netranasuaet* [cf. nasu?aitï? Wi 59]

shameful [adj] {vergonzoso} *netrarietrinasuet* [cf. nasu?aitï?, shame Wi 59]

shaving [n] {raspadura (de cualquiera cosa)} *tesibep* [cf. sibepï Wi 93]

sheep, domestic [n] {ganado lanar} *puejecuaré* [cf. pïhï, hair fuzz Wi 90; kwahaten, antelope Mi 115; pïhï ka-

bïrïï?, sheep (lit. "wooly goat") Wi 90]

shell of shellfish [n] {concha} *uacó* [wa?koo? Wi 147]

shepherd [n] {pastor} *chivaraibo* [cf. sippeh, sheep Mi 134; taiboo?, white man Wi 102]

shield [n] {chimal (adarga)} *pahquip* [cf. topï Wi 110]

shin [n] {espinilla} *cutzomó* [kutsi?omo Wi 32]

shirt [n] {camisa} *cuáso* [kwasu?u Wi 37]

shoe [n] {zapato} *nap* [napï Wi 56]

shoulder [n] {hombro} *jarauia* [error: *járacúa;** cf. huhkï, collarbone Wi 169]

shower, rain [n] {aguacero y también lluvia} *emar* [ïmaarï Wi 143]

sick [adj] {enfermo} *ueminahcat* [cf. wo'-me-nok-et, sickness De94 189]

sierra [n] {sierra} *piviayorabi* [error: *piviaroyabi;** cf. pia, big Wi 79; toyaabï, mountain Wi 112]

sigh [n] {suspiro} *nasauehquip* [cf. nasuawïhkitï Wi 59]

silver [n] {plata} *tosaui* [tosahwï Wi 111]

simple [adj] {sencillo} *cemanacbaco*

sing [v] {cantar} *tenicuaró* [tïnikwïrï, sing a song Wi 134]

sister, older [n] {hermana

mayor} *batzi* [cf. patsi?, eldest sister   Wi 77]; younger sister {hermana menor} *nami* [nami?   Wi 54]

sister-in-law, my   [n] (man speaking) {cuñada (del hombre)}   the same as **wife** [*cueh*]; (woman speaking) {cuñada (de la mujer) mi}   *neretz* [cf. nï, my   Wi 67; tets*i*, man's brother-in-law   Wi 107; paha piahpï, sister-in-law of a woman   Wi 74]

sit   [v] {sentarse}   *careró* [cf. kaht*i*   Wi 25]

six   [adj] {seis}   *nabaehté* [naabait*i*   Wi 49]

sixteen   [adj] {diez y seis}   *nabaehtematoequet* [nàh'-vite-àh-màh-to-y-kut   De94 97]

sixteenth   [adj] {décimosesto}   *netzasenoayacusivinacuyojé*

sixth   [adj] {sesto [sexto]}   *enesuatneseique*

sixty   [adj] {sesenta}   *nabachtémanri*

sixty-one   [adj] {sesenta y uno}   *nabachtémanri-cemamatoequet*

sixty-two   [adj] {sesenta y dos}   *nabachtémanri-nahtematoequet* and thus successively, repeating the expression meaning "sixty" and that meaning "thirteen," "fourteen," etc., up to "nineteen" {y así sucesivamente repitiendo la espresión que significa sesenta y las que significan trece, cotorce [catorce], etc., hasta diez y nueve}[8]

skillet   [n] {sartén}   *cuquemeauh* [kukïme?awe   Wi 31]

skin   [n] {cutis}   *tenepoá* [error: *jenepoá*; hïnïpo?a?, human skin   Wi 22]

skinny   [adj] {flaco}   *canabuehtzi* [cf. kanah, thin   Mi 111; -pittseh, noun suffix   Mi 20]

skull   [n] {cabeza (el cráneo)}   *tzohtáb* [cf. tsotso?neet*i*, rub head against something   Wi 1220]

skunk   [n] {zorrillo}   *nabohcutz* [cf. naboo-, marked, striped, spotted   Wi 50; kuutsu?, cow   Wi 32], *pisuhcuana* [cf. pisu:kwïrï'   Mc; Pisu kwá?na?, Smeller (derogatory band name)   Wi 82]

skunkbush [ill-scented sumac]   [n] {lantrisco}   *tahzip* [error: *tahtzip;** tatsïpï   Wi 105]

sky   [n] {cielo}   *tomóbi* [tomoob*i*, clouds, heaven   Wi 109]

sleep   [n] {sueño}   *ehpep* [cf. eepeiH, to sleep   Mi 107]; [v] {dormir}   *ehpueito* [ïhpïit*i*   Wi 142]

sleepwalker   [n] {sonámbulo}   *ehpuehcatzemiar* [cf. eepeiH, to sleep   Mi 107; mia, walk   Mi 118]

sly [adj] {disimulado}
noihquetenacat

small [adj] {chico (cosa pequeña)} *tiesuat* [cf. tïe Wi
128]; very small, tiny {chico
(muy), chiquito} *tiehteti,
tiehtetzi** [cf. tïtaatï, small
size, unworthy, pitied Wi
138]

smallpox [n] {viruelas} *tásia*
[tasiʔa? Wi 104]

smell [v] {oler} *ecuitó* [cf.
ekwiG Mi 107]

smoke [n] {humo} *cuip*
[kwipï Wi 38]; [v] {fumar}
pamuitan [cf. puha bahmuʔitï,
smoke during a religious
ceremony Wi 86; pahmu,
tobacco Wi 74]

snail [n] {caracol} *poná*

snake, water [n] {culebra del
agua} *pasinugia* [pasinnu-
yua Mi 128]

snakeweed [n] {cadillo} *soniuocué* [cf. sanaweha Ca
522]

sneeze [n] {estornudo} *acusé,
acusí* [akkwihsiG Mi 106]

snow [n] {nieve} *taahcábi*
[tahkabi Wi 100]

snuff [n] {rapé} *tzácusi* [cf.
tsaʔakusitï, (v) sneeze Wi
119]

soap [n] {jabón} *uanacótze*
[wana kotse? Wi 146]

soil [n] {suelo} *ohtabi*
[ohtapii Wi 72]

sole (of foot) [n] {planta (del
pie)} *tahpana* [tahpaana
Wi 101]

son [n] {hijo} *tua, rua* [tua?
Wi 123]; son (my) {hijo
(mi)} *nurua, netua* [cf. nï, my
Wi 67; tua?, son Wi 123]

son-in-law (my) [n] {yerno
(mi)} *nemonahpue* [cf. né,
my Wi 67; monahpï? Wi
46]

south [n] {sur} *yuané* [cf.
you'-a-nok De94 129]

sow bug [n] {cochinita [cochi-
nilla]} *ené* [ïnïʔ, bug, insect,
creature Wi 143; cf. kwita
maroapona Wi 38]

spades (card suit) [n] {espadas
(de la baraja)} *tahebebui*

speak [v] {hablar} *tecuaró*
[tekwarï Wi 107]

spider [n] {araña} *tatétz*
[tàh-tates' De94 125]

spine [backbone] [n] {espi-
nazo} *cuaiporop* [kwahipo-
ropï Wi 36]

spit [n] {asador} *tetzisteuei**
[cf. tïtsiwaii?, spear, sword
Wi 139]*

spit [v] {escupir} *tusitó* [tu-
sitï Wi 125]

spittle of a horse [n] {espuma
o baba del caballo} *sohcap*
[cf. yokapï, phlegm, juice
Wi 158]

spoon [n] {cuchara} *tiauó* [er-
ror: *tianó;** cf. ta'-nàh-ho,
pocket knife De94 192]

spring of water [n] {ojo de

agua} *patzaroehbenit-cuarehtecbenit* [cf. paa, water   Wi 73]; spring (first month) {primavera (la primera luna)} *equerámaro-chat, equerámarochcat** [cf. kwihne?, wintertime   Wi 38; tamarïkïkatï, completed   Wi 103]; spring (second month) {primavera (la segunda luna)} *equibuiseahcat* [cf. ek'-àh-nàh, before   De94:105; pui, green   Mi 131]; spring (third month) {primavera (la tercera luna)} *puiseahcat* [cf. pui, green   Mi 131]

spur [n] {acicate y también espuela} *pucseuhcueticó* [cf. puuk*u*, horse   Wi 88; pahparatsihkweetï, shiny   Wi 219]

spyglass [n] {anteojo} *tebu-juaé* [cf. tïpunirï, look at   Wi 136]

squirrel [n] {ardilla} *uocouoe* [wokoohwi   Wi 150]

stable [n] {caballariza} *pucú-cane* [puku kahni   Wi 88]

stand [v] {pararse} *ueneró* [cf. winïrï, standing (adj)   Wi 155]

star [n] {estrella} *tatzinupi* [tatsinuup*i*   Wi 105]

steamboat [n] {buque de vapor} *guobipúc-parú-miacuiguanámia, guobipuc-parumiaet cuiguianamiar** [cf. wobi puuk*u*, buggy, hack

(lit. "wood horse")   Wi 149; pa-, reference to water   Wi 73; mia, go   Mi 118]

steel (for starting fires)   [n] {eslabón (para sacar fuego)} *cósob* [cf. kaw'sawo, flint and steel to light fire with   De95 112]

still, calm [adj] {estar parado, quieto} *noihqueyúgüen;* sitting still {estar sentado, quieto} *noihqueyúcat* [cf. nohi, very Wi 65; ke- no, negative   Wi 27; yïkarï, walk, move about   Wi 159; kwe?yïkatï, tire out   Wi 38]

stilts [n] {zancos} *júmia* [cf. hu-, ref. to tree, wood, stick   Wi 20; mia, walk   Mi 118]

stink [v] {apestar} *tehtze-cuanar* [cf. tïtsï, bad   Wi 139; kwanarï, have odor   Wi 37]

stirrup [n] {estribo (de silla de montar)} *narahrtequí, narahtequí* [narahtïkii? (lit. "item to put foot in")   Wi 57]

stockings [n] {medias} *uan-anap* [wana nap*ï*   Wi 146]

straight [adj] {recto, derecho} *tunat* [cf. tuna   Wi 125]

strap [n] {correa} *picap* [cf. pikap*ï*, leather   Wi 81]

strawberry [n] {fresa} *ecah-pócope* [ekapokopi   Wi 15]

stretch [v] {estirar} *tzatunetzaró*

stupid [adj] {tonto} *saupaut*
[error: *suapuat;** cf. suap*ï*-
waht*ï* Wi 96]

suffer [v] {padecer}
quenenaveni

sugar [n] {azúcar} *pasina-
pihnab* [error: *pasiuapihnab;**
cf. pasi waap*i*, sand   Wi 77;
pihnáa?, sugar, sweets   Wi
81]; raw sugar loaf {pilon-
cillo} *pihnab* [pihnáa?, sugar,
sweets   Wi 81]

summer (first month) [n]
{verano (primera luna)}
puiseap [cf. pui, green   Mi
131]; summer (second month)
{verano (segunda luna)}
yebaroehcat [cf. yepani,
autumn   Mi 150]; summer
(third month) {verano (tercera luna)} *yebane, yebáne**
[cf. yepani, autumn   Mi 150]

sun [n] {sol} *taabe* [taabe
Wi 99]

sunrise [n] {sol saliente, la au-
rora} *taabetzaróehquit* [cf.
tabe to?ikit*ï*   Wi 99]

swallow [bird] [n] {golon-
drina} *pasocopi* [pasokom'-
pin   Mi 128]

sweat [n] {sudor} *tacusip*
[takw*ï*sip*ï*   Wi 103]

sweep [v] {barrer} *tenuaró*
[t*ï*ïnuar*ï*, sweep something
Wi 140]

swing [n] {columpio} *piguai-
sorve* [error: *piguaisoroe;** cf.

pi?wesuruu?*i*?, playground
swing   Wi 84]

T

tail [n] {cola (rabo)} *cuasi,
macuasi,** ucuase** [kwas*i*
Wi 37; ma, u, third-person
genitive pronouns   Wi 304];
[v] follow stealthily {colear}
temacuietó

tailbone [n] {rabadilla} *opi-
nosa* [error: *opiuosa;** cf.
piwo?s*a*   Wi 84]

take away [v] {quitar}
eyaquetoihné

tarantula [n] {tarántula} *ta-
puêhretz* [cf. p*ï*h*ï* re?ts*i*   Wi
90]

tear [lacrimal] [n] {lágrima}
ohpep [ohpep*ï*   Wi 225]

tear [v] {romper} *matzasiuró*
[masi?war*ï*, tear (by hand)
Wi 44]

teeth [n] {dientes} *muchitaama* [cf. mutsi-, pointed
Wi 48; tamm*a*, tooth   Wi
99]; set of teeth {dentadura}
taama [cf. taam*a*, tooth
Wi 99]

temple of the Comanches [n]
{templo de los Comanches}
piácane [pia, big   Wi 79;
kahni, house   Wi 24]

ten [adj] {diez} *cemanri* [cf.
sa'-im-en   De94 97]

tenth [adj] {décimo}
netzaivinacuyojé

testicle [n] {testículo} *onóyo*
[noyo   Mi 123]

that [pron] {aquel} *or* [cf.
ohri, orii   Wi 303]

there, at a distance, yonder
[adv] {allá}   *ocore* [cf. o-kï-
ho, (to) there   Wi 323]

these [pron] {éstos} *ite** [itïï
Wi 24], *itecuajip* [cf. itïkwï,
these two   Wi 24]

thief [n] {ladrón} *terehcá*
[tïrïhka?   Wi 137]

thigh [n] {muslo} *puicap*
[perk'-op, leg above knee
De94 80]

think [v] {saber y conocer}
osupanaet [cf. supana?itï,
knowing   Wi 96]

third [adj] {tercero} *eue-
suatmavinacure* [error:
enesuatmavinacure]

thirsty [adj] {sediento}
netzaracuhtiyiajuniar

thirteen [adj] {trece} *paistematoequet* [cf. pi'-hate-àh-
màh-to'-y-kut   De94 97]

thirteenth [adj] {décimotercio}
netzasémavinacuyojé

thirty [adj] {treinta} *paemanri* [cf. pi'-ha-men   De94
97]

thirty-one [adj] {treinta y uno}
paemanri-cemamatoequet

thirty-two [adj] {treinta y dos}
paemanri-nahtematequet and

thus successively repeating the
word for "thirty" and that
meaning "thirteen," "fourteen," etc., up to "nineteen"
{y así sucesivamente repitiendo la espresión que significa treinta y las que significan
trece, catorce, etc., hasta diez
y nueve}[9]

this [pron] {éste} *it* [itï
Wi 24]

thorn [n] {espina} *uocuebi*
[wokweeb*i*   Wi 150]

those [pron] {aquellos} *ore*
[ohrï, orïï   Wi 302]

thread (for sewing)   [n] {hilo
(para coser)} *uanaraneo* [er-
ror: *uanaram;** wana ramï
Wi 146]

three [adj] {tres} *paiste*
[cf. pahitï   Wi 74]

throw [v] {tirar} *uegquitó,
uistactó* [cf. kwihitï, throw
overhand   Wi 38]

thrush [n] {tordo (ave)} *cusisáe* [kusisai?, small gray bird
Wi 32]

thumb [n] {dedo pulgar}
mahtoc [mahtokoo?   Wi 40]

thunder [n] {trueno} *tomoyaquet* [tomoyaketï   Wi
110]

[thunderbird] Imaginary being
that they suppose is an extremely large bird with burning wings and that with its
crying produces the thunder

[n] {Ser imaginario que suponen una ave extremadamente grande, con las alas quemadas, y que con su llanto produce el trueno.} *tomouehtecua* [cf. tomo-, ref. to sky, cloud   Wi 109; t*a*ikwaG, to talk   Mi 136]

tick   [arachnid] [n] {garrapata} *caraa* [ka?ra?aa?   Wi 26]

tickle   [v] {[hacer] cosquillas} *pinaquetze* [cf. pinak*ï*ts*ïrï*, tickle someone   Wi 82]

tie   [v] {amarrar, atar} *mabuetzquenaró* [cf. n*ïï*ts*ï*k*ï*nar*ï*, tie up   Wi 70]

tinder   [n] {yesca} *nauatz* [cf. wattsi-ppeh   Mi 147]

tinkler (small bell)   [n] {cascabel} *oahuiaoujué, oajuicanojué** [error: *oahuicauojué*; cf. ohahpuhihwi, copper   Wi 71; kawohw*i*?, bell   Wi 26]

tired   [adj] {cansado} *cueyaehné* [cf. kwe?y*ï*kat*ï*, tire out   Wi 38]

toad   [n] {zapo [sapo]} *pasanao* [cf. p*à*h so we' yo   De94 124]

tobacco   [n] {tobaco} *pamo* [pahmu   Wi 74]

today   [adv] {hoy} *equihtzi* [cf. kihtsi?, now   Wi 28]

toe   [n] big toe {dedo gordo de pie} *tahtocó* [tahtokoo?   Wi 101]; second toe {dedo grande de pie} *tahcatz* [cf. tookaats*o*, toe   Wi 110];

third toe {dedo de enmedio del pie} *tahtevinat* [tahtïpinaa?, middle toe   Wi 102]; fourth toe {el mediano del pie} *tahtua* [tahtúa?, little toe   Wi 102]; little toe {el pequeño del pie} *tiehtahtua* [t*ï*eh tahtua? little toe   Wi 128]

tomorrow   [adv] {mañana (día prócsimo [próximo] venidero)} *puetze* [error: *puetzco;* * perts'-k De94 105]

tongue   [n] {lengua} *oecó* [eeko   Wi 16]

toothache   [n] {dolor de muelas} *taama nehtzicuar* [cf. taam*a*, tooth   Wi 99; n*ï*htsikwar*ï*, pain   Wi 67]

torch   [n] {hacha} *jujuandé* [cf. huu-, wood   Wi 20; weh'-had, blaze   De94 84]

trachea   [n] {traquearteria} *uororoqui* [wo?rorook*i* Wi 151]

tray   [n] {batea} *téson* [t*ï*soon*a*, pan, dishpan, plate Wi 138]

tree or wood   [n] {palo o madera} *júhpi* [huup*i* Wi 20]

triple   [adj] {triple} *paihnacbaco* [cf. pahit*ï*, three   Wi 74]

trunk [luggage]   [n] {baul} *uobióyote* [cf. wobi, ref. to wood   Wi 149; oyóot*i*?, parfleche   Wi 210]

turkey   [n] {pavo común} *cu-*

yoní [kuyu?nii Wi 33] *pui-cobe* [cf. puhitoo? Wi 87]

turkey vulture [n] {zopilote} *ecabapi* [ekabapi, red-headed buzzard Wi 162]

turtle [n] {tortuga} *uácani* [wakaree? Wi 145]

twelfth [adj] {duodécimo} *nesuatzá*

twelve [adj] {doce} *uahte-matoequet* [wàh'-hot-àh-màh-to'-y-kut De94 97]

twentieth [adj] {vigésimo} *netzarépinacuyojé*

twenty [adj] {veinte} *uah-manri, tocuenahmari* [error: *tocueuahmanri;* cf. tocucuah-manri;* wàh'-hà-màn De94 97]

twenty-first [adj] {vigésimo-primo} *netzarétibitri-cusicyujé*

twenty-one [adj] {veintiuno} *uahmanri-cemamatoequet*

twenty-two [adj] {veintidos} *uahmanri-uahtematoequet* and thus successively repeating the word for "twenty" and that meaning "thirteen," "fourteen," etc., up to "nineteen" {y así sucesivamente repitiendo la espresión que significa veinte y las que significan trece, catorce, etc., hasta diez y nueve}[10]

twist [v] {torcer} *marohpue-quetó* [cf. pikwebuitï, turn around quickly Wi 81]

two [adj] {dos} uah [waha Wi 144]

U

ugly [adj] {feo} *ayaquia, ayo*

umbrella [n] {paraguas} *jé-quiaé* [hïkiai Wi 22]

uncle [n] {tío} The same as **father** [ap]

undress oneself [v] {desnu-darse} *namacueyoitó* [cf. natsahkwe?yarï Wi 60]

urinate [v] {mear} *sito* [siitï Wi 93]

urine [n] {orines} *sip* [siipï? Wi 93]

V

vase, cup, jar [n] {copa, jarro y vasija} *tei-a-cararaibo*

vein [n] {vena} *upáe* [cf. pai Wi 73]

vermilion [n] {vermellon} *tá-bebisá** [cf. tabe-, sun Wi 99; cf. pisahpi, powder Wi 82; ekapisa?, rouge Wi 216]

very [n] {muy} *tibitzi* [te-pitsi, very Mi 140; cf. tïbitsi, really, surely Wi 127]

vest [n] {chaleco} *amacusó* [cf. ahma-wy-kkynah Cr 27; ana-, underarm Wi 12; kwasu?u, coat Wi 37]

viper [n] {víbora} *nújia* [nu-

hya?, snake of any species (ar-
chaic)   Wi 67]

vulva   [n]   {partes (las puden-
das de la muger [mujer])}   *táe*
[ta'ih, vagina   Mi 136]

W

wagon, long narrow   [n]   {ca-
rreta}   *juuobipuc* [cf. huu-,
wood   Wi 20; wobi puuku,
buggy, hack   Wi 149]

waist   [n]   {cintura}   *nanemea,
nanemuêa* [cf. nanema, *Bruste*
(breast, chest, bosom)   Be
51]

walk   [v]   {andar}   *nemitó*
[cf. nemiH, to move around
Mi 121]

wall   [n]   {pared}   *tepanabi*
[tïbanaa?   Wi 127]

walnut   [n]   {nuez (la de Cas-
tilla)}   *muvita* [mubitai   Wi
46]

warbonnet case   [n]   {saco ci-
líndrico con tapa para guar-
dar alguna cosa}   *tunahuosa*
[tuna wosa   Wi 125]

wasp, bee   [n]   {abeja, avispa}
pinahuárami [error: *pinah-
nárami;* cf. pihnaa?, sugar
Wi 81; narïmïï?, store   Wi
58]

water   [n]   {agua}   *paa* [paa
Wi 73]; icy water   {agua he-
lada}   *uehpahcaep* [epaak-
kappeh, ice   Mi 125]

watermelon   [n]   {sandía}
puihibinab [puhi bihnaa?
Wi 87]

we   [pron]   {nosotros}   *nen*
[nïnï   Wi 69]

web   [n]   {telaraña}   *uanaep*
[wana   Mi 147]

weep   [v]   {llorar}   *yaquetó* [cf.
yaketï, cry   Wi 157]

weeping   [adj]   {llorón}   *noyaquequia* [cf. yaketï, cry   Wi
157]

well [water]   [n]   {noria o pozo}
pahorap [pahorapï   Wi 74]

west   [n]   {poniente (el)}   *cahpinácuere* [kahpinakwï   Wi
25]

wheelbarrow   [n]   {carretela}
tieuobipuc [cf. tïe, small
Wi 128; wobi puuku, buggy,
hack   Wi 149]

wheel bug   [devil's riding horse]
[n]   {sisote}   *tosarae* [tosa-
rai?   Wi 111]

whip   [v]   {azotar}   *uchpaetó*
[cf. -paiH, to hit   Mi 126;
pian3'3pai'i, big whip
WH 271]

whirlwind   [n]   {remolino (de
viento)}   *ueabutzutzuit* [cf.
wer'-ah-werk-ee-tsu-ney
De94 133]

whiskey   [n]   {aguardiente}
poisabá [po?sa baa   Wi 86]

whistle   [n]   {pito}   *juhc* [cf.
huuk muyake   Wi 21]

white   [adj]   {blanco}   *tósabite*
[tosapïtï   Wi 111]; white flag

{bandera blanca} *tosanada-tzia* [cf. tosa-, white Wi 110; wana tsiyaa?, flag Wi 146]

white man or Mexican [n] {gente, o Mexicano} *tabebo, taibo, araibo* [cf. taiboo? Wi 102; yuu taibo?, Mexican (lit. "fat white man") Wi 159]

wide [adj] {ancho} *piauequité* [cf. pia, big Wi 79; wa*i*kih, so wide Mi 146]

wife [n] {muger [mujer]} *cueh* [kwïhï? Wi 39]

wildcat [n] {gato montés} *matzóhpe* [matïsohpe? Wi 161]

willow [n] {sauz} *sehêbi* [cf. sïhï Wi 97]

wind [n] {aire} *niet* [nïetï Wi 67]; {viento} *niehpi* [nïep*i* Wi 67]

wing [n] {ala} *ucás* [cf. kasa*a* Wi 26]

winter (first month) [n] {invierno (primera luna de)} *tómo* [cf. tommo, winter, year Mi 141]; winter (second month) {invierno (segunda luna de)} *tocuehtómo* [cf. tokweti, exact, proper Wi 109; tommo, winter, year Mi 141]; winter (third month) {invierno (tercera luna de)} *tómoramaroehcat, tómora-marohcat** [cf. tommo, winter, year Mi 141; tama-rïkïkati, completed Wi 103]

wipe [v] {limpiar} *mamachu-maró* [cf. matsumarï Wi 44]

wise [adj] {sabio} *queji-nauahtzit* [cf. kehena, nothing Wi 27; nasuwatsirï forget Wi 59]

witch, female [n] {bruja} *púha* [cf. puh*a*, medicine; puha?aitï, shaman Wi 86]

wolf [n] {lobo} *piaisa* [pia'isa Mi 129]

woman [n] {muger [mujer]} *guaihpe* [wa'ippe Mi 146]; old woman {anciana} *jebis-tzitzi, gebistzitzi** [hïbi tsiitsi? Wi 22]

wood [n] {madera} *júhpi* [huup*i* Wi 231]

woodpecker [n] {carpintero (ave)} *ecahcueré* ['ekakwïrï:', red hammer Mc]

worker [n] {trabajador} *quebisá*

worm [n] {gusano} *uoabi* [woa-pin Mi 149]

wrong [n] {tuerto} *totzo-conoet,* totzoeonoet* [cf. tïtsï-, cruel, mean, ugly, bad Wi 139]

Y

yawn [n] {bostezo (sustantivo)} *ehtam* [cf. ïhtamakï?atï (v) Wi 142]

yellow [adj] {amarillo} *ojapité* [cf. ohap*i*, yellow;

Ohap*iti* kwahi, Yellow-back (person's name)   Wi 71]

yes [adv] {sí} *jaa* [haa   Wi 17]

yesterday [adv] {ayer} *quéto* [kïtu   Wi 36]

you [sing. pron] {tú} *eu* [error: *en;** ïnï   Wi 143]; you [plural] {vosotros} *muem* [mïmi   Wi 49]

yours [adj, pron] {tuyo} *em,** *ema* [ï, ïmi, second-person-singular accusative pronoun, second form emphatic   Wi 303]

youth, male   [n] {joven varón)} *tuibitz* [tuibihtsi?   Wi 124]; female youth {joven (muger [mujer])} *tiehpuer* [tuepït   WH 145]

yucca [n] {lechuguilla} *isa-mumutzi* [cf. mumutsi?, yucca   Wi 47]

COMANCHE-ENGLISH VOCABULARY

A

aahtaqui locust
acuareit belch
acusé,* acusí sneeze
aguó glass
amacusó vest
amáfe underarm hair
amauó plum
anábi knoll
anaruhcat armpit
anicúra small ant
anicútz large red ant
animui fly
ap father, uncle
araibo Mexican or white man*
areca deer
arrab cheek
arrae bridle
atabitzanoyo button
  snakeroot*
auequebrahcuasi* (quequebrah-
  cuasi) kite
aui because*

ayaquia,* ayo ugly
ayarocueté four
ayarocuetémanri forty*
ayarocuetémanri-
  cemamatoequet forty-one*
ayarocuetematoéquet (ayaro-
  cueté-matoequet) fourteen
ayarocuetenacbaco quadruple*
ayo, ayaquia* ugly

B

bajitó fall*
batsi older sister*
bávi older brother*
bunitó look*

C

caa rat
caani house
cáco grandmother*

caé forehead
cahpinácuere west
cahpistoyopét* (cahpistóyopel) brain
cahtzáp,* cohtzap *atole*
caib eyebrow
canabuehtzi skinny*
canauocué cactus
caneaequicuató hand over
caraa tick
careró sit*
cauojué bell
cém ace
cemamatoequet eleven
cemanacbaco simple*
cemanouehminate nine
cemanouehminatemanri ninety*
cemanouehminatemanri-cemamatoequet ninety-one*
cemanoueminatematoequet nineteen
cemanri ten
cíen one*
cóbe mustang
cocorá chicken
coehquí return*
cohtzap, cahtzáp* *atole*
córohc necklace
cósob steel
cuahare* (cauhare) ram
cuaiporop spine
cuasehani *chical*
cuasi tail*
cuáso shirt
cuchtonaró burn*
cueh wife, sister-in-law (man speaking), woman*

cueuó dove
cueyaehné tired
cueyubó crown*
cuhtz buffalo
cuihné* (cuihué) north
cuip smoke
cuitaró defecate*
cujorá hoe
cuminé mole
cupitá candle
cuquemeauh skillet
cus pants
cusihcuá heron
cusimura female burro
cusisáe thrush
cusiuibi* (cusinobi) male burro
cutúbi coal
cutznanojicuató fight a bull*
cutzomó shin
cuuna fire
cuyoní turkey

CH

chaco glue
chahpaquito glue*
chiva goat
chivaraibo* (chixaraibo) shepherd
chucuhpua old man

E

ebihcuyonit roadrunner
ecabapi turkey vulture
ecacusayet light*
ecahchire chili

ecahcueré woodpecker

ecahcuitzet* (ecahaútzet) lightning

ecahpócope strawberry

ecapusia flea*

ecatzasabocá red blanket

ecauanap red cloth

ecauipes copper coin

ecjuhtzú cardinal

ecuitó smell*

eh ordinary poncho

ehpep sleep

ehpuehcatzemiar sleepwalker

ehpueito sleep*

ehtam yawn

ejeró cover oneself

em, ema* yours

emar rain, shower

en you

ené sow bug

enenaseique eighth*

enenaseiqueuên seventh

enesuativinacuere fourth*

enesuatmavinacure third*

enesuatneseique sixth*

equebitz new*

equebuiseahcat second month of spring

equenaqueto day before yesterday

equerámarochat,* equerámarochcat first month of spring

equeromhcal third month of autumn*

equeromhcat second month of autumn

equibuiseahcat second month of spring

equihtzí now, today

ereit heat

esiavit Milky Way

et bow

eteaé mulberry

etzapuinit cross-eyed

etzeit cold

etzip ash

evivit blue

eyacraitoihné rob, take away*

G

gebistzitzi, jebistzitzi* old woman

goineroibo musician*

guaihpe woman

guaihputzarua offspring

guanarohpeté deck of cards

guasápe black bear

güêa penis

guobipúc-parúmiacuiguanámia,* guobipucparumiaet cuiguianamiar steamboat

guobiuihtua Indian drum

I

icaro enter*

icmitz very close

inap jerky

iquite here

isamumutzi yucca

isap liar

it this

ite   these
itecuajip   these
ivinacuyohené   fifth*

J

jaa   yes
jábi   pocketknife
jabitó   lie*
janib   corn
janibaraibo   farmer*
janibihtauorá   corncob*
janibitapuip   leaf of ear of corn
janiquetó   promise*
janitó   do*
járacúa   shoulder
jebistzitzi,* gebistzitzi   old
  woman
jeihtetzi   few
jenepoá   skin*
jéni   hiccup
jequiacat   shadow
jéquiaé   umbrella
jéyiu   much
jibito   drink*
jimatác   hardly
jonobitz   bat
jotoco   back
jucáhpi   reed
jucuni* (jucúm)   quiver
juhc* (juhe)   whistle
júhcup   dust
júhpi   tree, wood
juhpuc   crutch
juhtziscá   saw
juhtzú   bird
juhtzu a caané   nest

jujuandé   torch
júmia   stilts
junacoroito   leave*
junáu* (junun)   porcupine
junubi-pucúcane   corral
juuobipuc   long narrow wagon

M

ma   his, hers, its
mábat   above
mabuecuitzonobó   entangle*
mabuetzquenaró   tie*
macamaquetó   desire, love*
macuasi   tail
mahcatz   ring finger
mahpána* (mahpá)   palm
mahquitzaná   chameleon*
mahtevinat   middle finger
mahtoc   thumb
mahtua   little finger
mahtzahtema   close*
mamachumaró   wipe*
manacuré   far
marepetranicaró   curb*
marido   husband*
maritanahcat   send*
marohpuequetó   twist*
maruhcát   below
masihtó   fingernail
maténicue   Adam's apple
matocuehtevinauequico   half*
matzasiuró   tear*
matzitjuaró   open*
matzocá   fist
matzóhpe   wildcat
mauchpar   extend*

mavinacure   second*
mavuearó   loosen*
mayahcuató   carry*
mayaque   bring*
miar   go*
mihtetzi   near
míhtzi* (méhtzi)   ankle
moo   hand
moobeté   five
moobetémanri   fifty*
moobetémanri-cemamatoequet
   fifty-one
moobetematoequet   fifteen
motz   beard
motzinica   ring
movetenacbaco   quintuple*
muchicua   mosquito
muchitaama   teeth
muea   moon
muem   you
muitar   turned-up nose
mumutzi   palm
mumutziapocope   date*
mupitz   owl
murahcát   down*
muranáqui   maguey
murauar   aquiline nose
murayáque* (marayáque)
   bullfrog
murraé   kiss
muvi   nose
muviporo   pig
muvisip   mucus
muvita   walnut*
muvitaet   nostril
muviyehpap   flat-nosed
muyienaet   east
muyietaet   door

N

nabac   bullet
nabacaet   lead
nabachtémanri   sixty*
nabachtémanri-cemamatoequet
   sixty-one*
nabachtémanri-nahtematoequet
   sixty-two*
nabaehté   six
nabaehtematoequet   sixteen
nabohcutz   skunk
naboné   mirror
naboróyarohco   jaguar
nabuniquit   dawn*
nabusiaep   dream*
nacobetzanica   mask*
nacusi* (nucusi)   pumpkin
nacútusí,* nácutzi   gunpowder
nafoaiuape   doctor*
najoiquite   belt*
namacueyoitó   undress*
namaréma   ceiling, door, roof
nameuatzeuhté   eight
nameuatzeuhtémanri   eighty*
nameuatzeuhtemanri-
   cemamatoequet   eighty-one*
nameuatzeuhtenatoequet
   eighteen
nami   younger sister*
namsuaró   dress
namunacure   first*
nanauchtiuehquitó   compare*
nanemea, nanemuêa*   waist
nanemucahcacat   detain*
nanevecaetó   equal*
naoquit   rejoice*
nap   shoe

naparaibo cobbler*
napé foot
naquehtábae pecan
náqui ear
naquitaet* (naquitael) hearing
naquitárauet hole in ear for
   earring
naquitzáuacoa earring
narahrtequí,* narahtequí
   stirrup
narehcá meal
narenó saddle
nárso leather bag
nasauehquip sight
naséca persimmon tree
nasehpé ball*
natramuese grape*
natzahcuinó pistol
natzamucoe grape
natziminá crook, joint
natzistuya brush made from
   agave
nauatz tinder
nautoró give*
navitequetó quarrel*
ne I
nea my
nebaep calm*
nebahpiap my daughter-in-
   law*
nebáve older brother
necobetzanica headstall
necoco my grandmother*
negünitó hang*
nehetzauá fan
nehotzoquitaen small pot
néhtzisque scissors
nehutzipiap father-in-law*

nejuhcutaen clavicle
nemencaco my mother-in-law
   (man speaking)*
nementóco father-in-law*
neminoet owl
nemitó walk*
nemonahpue my son-in-law*
nemunácuere from ahead
nen we
nenamuiecap my clothing
nénap chest*
neneyeue alligator
neoihninacure left
nequenotzine great-
   grandchildren*
nequet crane
nerámi younger brother*
nerenorequitó saddle*
nerete my niece*
neretz my brother-in-law (man
   speaking), my sister-in-law
   (woman speaking)*
neririeté my family*
nerivitzinacure right
neroco my grandfather, my
   grandchild*
nerua, netua my son, my
   nephew
nesuatraicyujé eleventh*
nesuatzá twelve*
netoco my grandfather, my
   grandchild*
netranasuaet shame*
netrarietrinasuet shameful*
netua, nurua my son*
netzaicyujé ninth*
netzaivinacuyojé tenth*
netzaracuhtiviajuniar thirsty*

netzarépinacuyojé twentieth*

netzarétibitricusicyujé twenty-
first*

netzaribitzayacusicuyoje nine-
tieth*

netzaseayacuasicyojé seven-
tieth*

netzaseinonaiá fortieth*

netzasémavinacuyojé thirtieth*

netzasenoayacusivinacuyojé
sixtieth*

netzasenomavinacuyojé fif-
tieth*

netzasetibitzayacusicuyoje
eightieth*

nevia my mother

nevinácuere from behind

neyahipue my mother-in-law
(woman speaking)*

niatz no

niehpi wind

niet air, wind

nihcaró dance*

noetzitzanica saddle pad

nohito deceive*

noihquetenacat sly*

noihqueyúcat sitting still*

noihqueyuguen still*

nojitó play*

nójo before*

noró haul

noróhnap bed

noyaehbenit boil

noyaquequia weeping

nóyo bird egg

nuhquitó run*

nújia viper

nurua, netua my son*

O

oá horn

oajuicauojué* (oajuicanojué)
tinkler (small bell)

oajuimauitzohc metal bracelet

oania* (uania) mane

oaui gold

oauipes gold coin

ocore there

ocuebi Rio Grande

ocuebocopi prickly pear

oecó tongue

oguáhtze rib

ohpep tear

ohtabi soil

ojapité yellow, gold coins

ojótoco flank

omacuiyaró frighten*

omo leg

omocamacat leg pain

oná baby*

ona saltpeter*

onabi salt

onem liver

onibuecacát cold

onip cough

onoit crooked

onóyo testicle

ooa screech or barn owl

opés coin

opíh heart

opiuosa tailbone

opuer arm

opúi gall

or that

ore those

osacurauoar pelt

osíco   navel
osom, osomo*   lung
osupanaet   know*
oteauh   gourd
otuh   marrow
oyiuh   fat
oyote   parfleche

P

paa   water
pabohtoc   buttock
pabotabebo   North American
pac   arrow
pacandé   arrows
paêmá   rainspell
paemanri   thirty*
paemanri-cemamatoequet
     thirty-one*
paemanri-nahtematequet
     thirty-two*
pagüenér   high*
pahcusó   cassock*
pahopi   hail*
pahorap   well
pahquip   shield
paihnacbaco   triple*
paiste   three
paistematoequet   thirteen
pajabito   bathe*
pamo   tobacco
pamoe   bulrush, maguey stalk
pamouetz   beaver
pamuitan   smoke
panacuerehtep   lip
papi   head hair
papicamacat   headache*

papiguaght   bald
papituhtzaep   dandruff*
papiuehtáma   otter, cord to tie
     hair
parahpaet   downpour*
paraibocusó   cassock*
páretz   chin
parocoa   rainbow
parumíaet   sailboat
pasanao   toad*
pasauiyió   frog
pasibunaet   drizzle*
pasinugia   water snake
pasiuape   sand
pasiuapihnab   sugar
pasocopi   swallow
patzaroehbenit-cuarehtecbenit
     spring*
patzinacuse   fine poncho
patzohuip   drop*
pécui   fish
pehcaró   kill*
pia* (piab)   mother
piácane   temple of the
     Comanches
piaet   carbine, rifle
piaguoin   bugle
piaisa   wolf
piajuhtzu   eagle
piajunubi   large arroyo, river
piamupitz   ogre
piápre   big
piarabo   hare
piarama   molar
piauequite   wide
picamauitzohc   bracelet of hide
picap   strap
piguaisoroe   swing

pigusoa   saddlebag
pihiande   young boys
pihiboa   robe
pihnab   raw sugar loaf
pihpitz   horsefly
pihpó   belly
pijura   bean
pimaró   cattle
pinacuerenapuetzco   day after
   tommorrow*
pinahnárami   bee, wasp
pinaquetze   tickle
pinarusup   pinole
pínica   petticoat
pisibui   lacrimal sand
pisip   pus
pisuhcuana   skunk
pisup   flatulence
pitzi   woman's breast
pitzip   milk
pitzip-a-namarrivap   cheese*
piviarama   molars
piviaronap   peach
piviaroyabi   sierra
poap   tree bark
pocope   fruit*
pohpitó   jump
poisá   crazy
poisabá   whiskey
poná   snail
póro   bar of iron
puácane   church
puc   horse
pucseuhcueticó   spur*
pucúcane   stable
pucugüehpaé   quirt
pucurua   colt
pué   road

puehpi   blood
puêjap   hair*
puejecuaré   sheep
puêr   arm*
puerahcamacat   arm pain
pueratzuqui   biceps
puetep   old*
puetzco   tomorrow
puetzconacuere   morning
pueye   duck
púha   witch
púi   eye
puicap   thigh
puicobe   turkey
puiguat   blind*
puihgüi   iron
puihguioteauh   bottle
puihgüitzisca* (paihgüitzisca)
   file
puihibinab   watermelon
puinars   eyelid
puiseahcat   third month of
   spring
puiseap   first month of summer
pursi   eyelash
pusia   louse
pusiarachi   nit
puyiauh   tin cup

Q

quebisá   worker*
quehenanesuaet   happy*
quehetza   nothing
quehtanet   hurricane
quêhtzi   canine tooth
quehtziaró   bite*

quejinauahtzit   wise*
quenábunit   darkness
quenenaveni   suffer*
querajú   hackberry tree
quesuat   rude
quetécuahcat   mute
quetenacat   deaf
quéto   yesterday
quimaró   come*
quip   elbow

R

rámi   younger brother*
róco   grandfather*
rua   son*

S

sabahpáqui   drum
sahtotzip   foam of water; flower
   in general*
sahtotziyiab* (sahtotziyiar)
   flower of the wild palm
saitinereneyaquenoqui   charge*
sanahcó   chewing gum
sanahpi   gum
sapayé   javelina
sarrie   dog
seêhpet   even
sehêbi   willow
senoé   feather outfit
sia   feather
sip   urine
sito   urinate*
socobí   land*

soeoauh (socoauh)   *copas*
soeoauó (socoauó)   jug
sóhcap   foam or spittle of horse
sohobocopi   mulberry tree
sómaet   fold
sóna   bedspread
sonip   grass
soniuocué   snakeweed*
soomó* (soanió)   centipede
sot   much
sóte   Pleiades
soyáque   mockingbird
suabeaep   cross
suapuat   stupid
suatzá   also
subecatecua   hush*
sucuitae   owe
súji   pubic hair
suparello, supareyos   hat

T

taabe   sun
taabetzaróehquit   sunrise
taahcábi   snow
taahpue   God
taama   set of teeth
taame nehtzicuar,*
      taamenehtzicuar   toothache
tábebisa   vermillion
tabebo   Mexican or white man
tabecusé   date
tábo   rabbit, Big Dipper
tacusip   sweat
táe   vulva
taen   anus
taet   hole

tahc* (tahe)   arrowhead
tahcatz   second toe
tahebebui   spades*
tahpana   sole*
tahpicó   heel
tahtatzinupi   morning star
tahtevinat   third toe
tahtocó   big toe
tahtua   fourth toe
tahtzeuhte   seven*
tahtzeutematoequet   seventeen*
tahtzip   skunkbush
taibo   Mexican or white man,
   jack
taiboahpi   yellow*
taibobicap   leather
taibobinap   melon
taibobuihpi   blue*
taibouiahpe   king*
tamaruhc   gums
tamasual   first month of
   autumn*
támo   nerve
tamutzoe   brier
tandap   knee
tapuêheretz   tarantula
tarenamó   guards
tariguanap* (taraguanap)
   cloth
tásia   smallpox
tatétz   spider
tatoco   God
tatzeuhté   seven
tatzeuhtematoequet   seventeen
tatzinupecabit, tatzinupecahpi
   comet
tatzinupi   star
tatzinupi-bajin   ray of light

tatzinupi-puetuhcatutamiae
   North Star
tauitz   calf
tayáque   rooster
teboet   painter*
tebor   paint*
tebujuaé   spyglass
techiaroihp   acid indigestion*
teconicaquetó   rope*
teconiuap   brave
tecuaró   speak*
tehcap   meat
tehcaró   eat*
tehei   horse
tehtzecuanar   stink*
tei-a-cararaibo   cup, jar, vase
tejeiania   horse's mane
temacuatui   paper
temacuietó   tail*
temuecuató   buy*
temuer   sell*
temumuquit   hummingbird
tenacaró   hear*
tenahpua   man
tenicuaró   sing*
tenisúyaet   jeer
tenuaró   sweep*
tep   mouth
tepanabi   wall
tequeuehtiap   garbage
tequiheató   hold*
terehcá   thief
têsahta   bread
tesibep   shaving
téson   tray
tetanahcat   poor
tetanasuat   sadden*
tetecae   flint

tetzabor   scatter*
tetzahquená   awl
tetzasquenaró   sew*
tetziscaró   cut*
tetzisteuei   spit
tetzitzúca   index finger
tetzocuetó   grind*
tetzóteuei   plowman*
teyaep   corpse
tianó   spoon
tibitzi   very
tibitzi-piaocuebi   sea
tiehpuer   female youth
tiehtahtua   fifth
tiehteti,* tiehtetzi   very small, tiny
tiehtoyábi   little hill
tienobipuc   wheelbarrow
tiesuat   small
tieuegquité   narrow*
tieuehquitetzi* (tienehquitetzi) very narrow
tiohnab   loose
tirehbasú   partridge
tiremuchicua   mosquito
tiriejuhtzú   any small bird
tocoehcatz   first month of autumn
tocuehtaben   noon
tocuehtatz   second month of autumn*
tocuehtómo   second month of winter
tocuehtucan   midnight*
tocueuahmanri* (tocucuahmanri) twenty
tocusé   no*

tohpana   sole of the foot
tói   pipe*
toito   mount*
tómo   first month of winter
tomoahcat   cloudy
tomóbi   sky
tomohcat   third month of autumn
tómoramarohcat   third month of winter
tomorarauet* (temorarauet) cloud
tomouehtecua   Thunderbird
tomoyaquet   thunder
toroponí   potato
tósabite   white
tosagüera   white bear
tosanadatziá   white flag*
tosanebaehcap, tosanebaep frost
tosarae   wheel bug
tosarecá   Mexican deer
tosasabocá   white blanket
tosaui   silver
tosauipes   silver coin
totzeuhtemanri   seventy*
totzeuhtemanri-cemamatoequet seventy-one*
toyábi   hill
toyarohco* (toyorohco)   cougar
toyop   neck
tozoconoet, totzoeonoet*   wrong
tua   son
tuaahtaqui   cricket
tucan   night
tuhcanacuerehtep   lip
tuhpaé, tupaé*   coffee

tuhpísi* (tuhpúi) Negro
tuhtzaep dirt, scab
tuhtzanoyoit dirty
tuhubit black color
tuibitz male youth
tuinéhpua boy
tujuhpi evergreen oak
tujuicá crow
tunahuosa warbonnet case
tunat straight
tunayó black bear
tunequi heron
turuhpi black pigment*
tusip saliva
tusitó spit*
tuttzaiuat clean
tutzi grandson*
tuure leech

TZ

tzácusi snuff
tzanábunit light
tzanahcat rich
tzanicá breechcloth
tzat good
tzatunetzaró stretch*
tzena coyote
tziareyiajumiar hungry*
tzie* (tzic) lance
tzóhpe pillow
tzohpoá scalp*
tzohtáb skull
tzómeto join*
tzoom bead
tzotzone cramp

tzuhnip bone*
tzuninatzistuya*
(tzuninatzishtuya) comb

U

uácani turtle
uacatz all*
uacó shell
uah two
uahmanri twenty*
uahmanri-cemamatoequet
twenty-one*
uahmanri-uahtematoequet
twenty-two*
uahtematoequet twelve
uanacbac double
uanácotz soap
uanaep web
uananap stockings
uanaram (uanaraneo)* thread
uanatzahquená needle
uanatziá flag*
uanauósa cloth bag
uao cat
uatzavitó hide oneself*
ucás wing
uchpaetó whip*
ucuase tail
ucubisi brains
ucuitatz intestine
ucuma male
ucútz gullet
ueabutzutzuit whirlwind
uegquitó throw*
uehpahcaecat ice*

uehpahcaep icy water
uehquétzutzu rattle
uehtuné pieces of jerky
ueminahcat sick*
ueneró stand*
uequitzóhpe headboard
ueto go down*
uétzi gray hair
ueyahcoró butterfly
ui knife
uihtuabape hat
uinaét lame
uistactó throw*
uistúa bucket
uiyá halter, lariat
uoabi worm
uobióyote trunk
uobipihuab honey
uóbipuc carriage
uocouoe squirrel
uocuebi thorn
uohtzauet roughness

uohué mesquite
uoniayaquep gum
uororoqui trachea
upáe vein
upiab female
upúi gall*
usihcop scapula

yahnet laugh
yaquetó weep*
yebane third month of summer
yebaroehcat second month of summer
yeihca afternoon
yeinácuere darken
yetzeró rise*
yocoró limp*
yuané south
yuup fat

NOTES

1. Pimentel actually made the proposed comparisons in the second volume of a three-volume expanded edition of *Lenguas Indígenas* (1874–1875:2:25–44).

2. Cuatrociénegas de Carranza, Coahuila.

3. Only some of the groups are Comanche; the rest occupied adjacent territories and knew Comanche as a regional trade language. Yaparehca, Cuhtzuteca, Penande, and Noconi are versions of four widely reported Comanche division names. Yapaine is not a separate group as indicated but a synonym for Yaparehca. The identification of the Noconi division with the distinct Yiuta (Ute) tribe is incorrect. The Kiowas are listed twice, as Caiguaras and Caigua. Pacarabo and Sianabore are both Comanche names for the Cheyennes ("striped arrow" and "striped feather," respectively), while Sarritehca, a Shoshonean term meaning "dog-eater," most likely denotes the Arapahoes during this period (though Thurman [1988] has raised the possibility that it could denote Athapaskan remnants living among the Comanches). Napuat, "shoeless" in Comanche, was applied to the populations of the lower Rio Grande valley referred to by the Spanish collectively as Carrizos. García Rejón's equation of Napuat with Quetahtore has been perpetuated (e.g., via Pimentel in Hodge 1907), but could not be verified independently. Quetzaene resembles the Comanche term for Pawnees, Kuitaraine ("buttocks"), reported by Gatschet (1884:65, 121) and Scott (1897). Muvinabore ("marked [striped, spotted] noses" in Comanche) is not documented elsewhere,

but probably is an alternate for *na'somoni'hta* or "ring nose" (Gatschet 1884:121), used for the Caddos, apparently because of "their peculiar fashion of suspending various jewels from the septum of the nose" (Berlandier 1969:52, 159).

4. Linguists now recognize that in Comanche "there are apparently no tense markers as such, but a rich array of aspect markers. Tense refers to specification of when, in the flow of time, an event takes place. Aspect does not place an event in time, but rather focuses on other features of the event—its beginning or ending, whether it is ongoing or not, whether it is to be considered as an action or as a state, and so on" (Wistrand-Robinson and Armagost 1990:314). In discussing the preterit imperfect, García Rejón probably refers to the aspect suffix *-yu*, "continuous" (Miller 1972:17), and his preterit perfect example seems to report the aspect suffix interpreted as *-ppeh*, "perfective" (ibid.) or *-ppyh*, "absolutive" (Crapo 1976:73). His instructions for the future tense do not conform to his example; Pimentel (1874–1875:2:18) tried unsuccessfully to clarify the example by rearranging the instructions. Most likely García Rejón intended to show the aspect suffix for indefinite future, rendered *-nuhi* by Miller (1972:17) and Crapo (1976:7).

5. In Numic counting systems, the term glossed as "eleven" actually means "one more than the last decade counted"; "twelve" is actually "two more than the last decade counted"; and so on. Thus "eighty-two" in Comanche is explained as a compound of "eighty" and "twelve"; "eighty-three" in Comanche is explained as a compound of "eighty" and "thirteen"; and so on.

6. See note to entry eighty-one.

7. See note to entry eighty-one.

8. See note to entry eighty-one.

9. See note to entry eighty-one.

10. See note to entry eighty-one.

11. The Comanche words in parentheses are the variations or misspellings that appeared somewhere in the original 1866 edition; the main entries are the correct spellings. The asterisks mark words that did not appear in the original Comanche-Spanish section.

BIBLIOGRAPHY

Alvarez, José Rogelio, dir.
   1971   García Rejón, Lic. Manuel. In *Enciclopedia de México*, 5:
          392. Mexico City, Enciclopedia de México, S.A.

Anonymous
   1959   Dedication: Chief Wild Horse Headstone. *Chronicles of
          Comanche County* 5(3):58–66.

Arroyo, José Miguel
   1865   Reseña de los trabajos científicos de la Sociedad Mexicana
          de Geografía y Estadística en el año de 1864. In *Boletín de
          la Sociedad Mexicana de Geografía y Estadística*, 1ª época,
          11:3–27.
   1866   Reseña de los trabajos científicos de la Sociedad Mexicana
          de Geografía y Estadística en el año de 1865. In *Boletín de
          la Sociedad Mexicana de Geografía y Estadística*, 1ª época,
          12:4–55.

Barnard, Herwanna Becker
   1941   The Comanche and His Literature. Master's thesis, Uni-
          versity of Oklahoma.

Becker, W. J.
   1931   The Compounding of Words in the Comanche Indian Lan-
          guage. Master's thesis, University of Oklahoma.
   1936   The Comanche Indian and His Language. *Chronicles of
          Oklahoma* 14:328–342.

Berghaus, Heinrich Karl Wilhelm
   1851   *Physikalischer Atlas: Geographische Jahrbuch zur Mittheilung aller wichtigern neuen Erforschungen.* Vol. 3. Gotha: Justus Perthes.

Berlandier, Jean Louis
   1969   *The Indians of Texas in 1830.* Washington, D.C.: Smithsonian Institution Press.

Bollaert, William
   1956   *William Bollaert's Texas.* Norman: University of Oklahoma Press.

Brice, Donaly E.
   1987   *The Great Comanche Raid.* Austin: Eakin Press.

Campbell, T. N., and William T. Field
   1968   Identification of Comanche Raiding Trails in Trans-Pecos Texas. *West Texas Historical Association Year Book* 44: 128–144.

Canonge, Elliott
   1958   *Comanche Texts.* Norman, Oklahoma: Summer Institute of Linguistics.

Cárdenas Villareal, Carlos
   1977   *Aspectos culturales del hombre nomada de Coahuila.* Saltillo: Colegio Coahuilense de Investigaciones.
   1978   Aspectos culturales del hombre nomada de Coahuila. *Revista Coahuilense de Historia* 1(3):40–50.

Carlson, Gustav G., and Volney H. Jones
   1939   Some Notes on Uses of Plants by the Comanche Indians. *Papers of the Michigan Academy of Science, Arts, and Letters* 25:517–542.

Catlin, George
   1973   *Letters and Notes on the Manners, Customs, and Conditions of the Indians of North America.* Vol. 2. New York: Dover Publications [orig. 1844].

Cavazos Garza, Israel
   1984   García Rejón, Manuel. In *Diccionario Biográfico de Nuevo León.* 1:172–173. Monterrey: Universidad Autónoma de Nuevo León.

Conger, Roger N., et al.
   1966   *Frontier Forts of Texas.* Waco: Texian Press.

Corwin, Hugh D.
 1959 *Comanche and Kiowa Captives in Oklahoma and Texas.*
    Lawton, Oklahoma: Hugh D. Corwin.
Crapo, Richley H.
 1976 *Big Smokey Valley Shoshoni.* Desert Research Institute
    Publications in the Social Sciences 10. Logan: Utah State
    University.
Detrich, Charles H.
 1894 Comanche Vocabulary. Manuscript, National Anthropo-
    logical Archives.
 1895 Comanche-English Dictionary and Vocabulary of Phrases.
    Manuscript, Western History Collections, University of
    Oklahoma.
Diccionario Porrua de Historia, Biografía, y Geografía de México
 1976a García Rejón y Carvajal, Joaquín. Pp. 831–832. Mexico
    City: Editorial Porrua, S.A.
 1976b García Rejón y Mazo, Manuel. P. 832. Mexico City: Edi-
    torial Porrua, S.A.
Dolbeare, Benjamin
 1986 *A Narrative of the Captivity and Suffering of Dolly Web-
    ster among the Camanche Indians of Texas.* New Haven:
    Yale University Library.
Flores, Dan
 1991 Bison Ecology and Bison Diplomacy: The Southern Plains
    from 1800 to 1850. *Journal of American History* 78:
    463–485.
Follett, C. R.
 1938 *Oldham County, Texas: Records of Wells and Springs.*
    Miscellaneous Publications of the Texas Water Commis-
    sion No. 199. Austin: State Board of Water Engineers.
Fowler, Don D., and Catherine S. Fowler, eds.
 1971 *Anthropology of the Numa: John Wesley Powell's Manu-
    scripts of the Numic Peoples of Western North America,
    1868–1880.* Smithsonian Contributions to Anthropology
    14. Washington, D.C.: Smithsonian Institution Press.
García Rejón, Manuel
 1865 Vocabulario del idioma Comanche. *Boletín de la Sociedad
    Mexicana de Geografía y Estadística,* 1ª época, 11:631–
    659. Reprinted Mexico City: Ignacio Cumplido, 1866.

Gatschet, Albert S.

  1884   Comanche Vocabulary and Notes. Manuscript, National Anthropological Archives.

Gelo, Daniel J.

  1989a   Comanche Animal Classifications. Paper presented at the annual meeting, American Anthropological Association, Washington, D.C.

  1989b   Comanche Fieldnotes. Manuscript.

  1993   The Comanches as Aboriginal Skeptics. *American Indian Quarterly* 17:69–81.

Gladwin, Thomas

  1948   Comanche Kin Behavior. *American Anthropologist* 50: 73–94.

Greene, A. C.

  1972   *The Last Captive.* Austin: Encino Press.

Hill, Jane H.

  1992   The Flower World of Old Uto-Aztecan. *Journal of Anthropological Research* 48:117–144.

Hodge, Frederick Webb, ed.

  1907   *Handbook of American Indians North of Mexico.* 2 vols. Bureau of American Ethnology Bulletin 30. Washington, D.C.: U.S. Government Printing Office.

Jackson, A. T.

  1938   *Picture Writing of Texas Indians.* Publication 3809. Austin: University of Texas.

Jones, David E.

  1972   *Sanapia: Comanche Medicine Woman.* New York: Holt, Rinehart and Winston.

  1980   Face the Ghost. *Phoenix* 4:53–57.

Jones, Oakah L., Jr.

  1988   *Nueva Viscaya: Heartland of the Spanish Frontier.* Albuquerque: University of New Mexico Press.

Kavanagh, Thomas

  1986   Political Power and Political Organization: Comanche Politics, 1786–1875. Doctoral dissertation, University of New Mexico.

Keyser, James D.

  1987   A Lexicon for Historic Plains Indian Rock Art: Increasing Interpretive Potential. *Plains Anthropologist* 32:43–71.

Kirkland, Forrest, and W. W. Newcomb, Jr.
1967   *The Rock Art of Texas Indians.* Austin: University of Texas
         Press.
McAllester, David P.
1940   Comanche Field Notes. Manuscript in editor's possession.
Mallery, Garrick
1881   Sign Language among North American Indians. In *Bureau
         of American Ethnology First Annual Report,* ed. J. W.
         Powell. Pp. 269–550. Washington, D.C.: U.S. Government
         Printing Office.
1893   *Picture Writing of the American Indians.* Bureau of Ameri-
         can Ethnology Tenth Annual Report. Washington, D.C.:
         U.S. Government Printing Office.
Mayhall, Mildred P.
1962   *The Kiowas.* Norman: University of Oklahoma Press.
Miller, Wick R.
1972   *Newe Natekwinappeh: Shoshoni Stories and Dictionary.*
         Anthropological Papers 94. Salt Lake City: University of
         Utah.
Mooney, James
1896   *The Ghost Dance Religion and Sioux Outbreak of 1890.*
         Bureau of American Anthropology Fourteenth Annual Re-
         port, Part 2. Washington, D.C.: U.S. Government Printing
         Office.
Osborn, Henry, and William A. Smalley
1949   Formulae for Comanche Stem and Word Formation. *In-
         ternational Journal of American Linguistics* 15:93–99.
Parsons, Mark L.
1987   Plains Indian Portable Art as a Key to Two Texas Historic
         Rock Art Sites. *Plains Anthropologist* 32:257–274.
Pimentel, Francisco
1862–   *Cuadro descriptivo y comparativo de las lenguas indíge-
1865   nas de México, o tratado de filología mexicana.* 2 vols.
         Mexico City: Imprenta de Andrade y Escalante.
1874–   *Cuadro descriptivo y comparativo de las lenguas indí-
1875   genas de México, o tratado de filología mexicana.* Se-
         gunda edición única completa. 3 vols. Mexico City: Isi-
         doro Epstein.

Plummer, Rachel

1977 *Rachel Plummer's Narrative.* Austin: Jenkins Publishing Company [orig. 1838].

Richardson, Rupert N.

1933 *The Comanche Barrier to South Plains Settlement.* Glendale, California: Arthur A. Clark.

Rister, Carl Coke

1989 *Comanche Bondage.* Lincoln: University of Nebraska Press [orig. 1955].

St. Clair, H. H., and Robert H. Lowie

1909 Shoshone and Comanche Tales. *Journal of American Folklore* 22:265–282.

Sapir, Edward

1931 Southern Paiute Dictionary. *Proceedings of the American Academy of Arts and Sciences* 65:537–730.

Schilz, Jodye Lynn Dickson, and Thomas F. Schilz

1989 *Buffalo Hump and the Penateka Comanches.* El Paso: Texas Western Press.

Schoolcraft, Henry Rowe

1851– *Historical and Statistical Information respecting the History, Conditions, and Prospects of the Indian Tribes of the United States.* 6 vols. Philadelphia: Lippincott and Grambo.
1857

Scott, Hugh Lenox

1897 Indian Sign Language Notes. Manuscript, U.S. Army Field Artillery and Fort Sill Museum Library, Lawton, Oklahoma.

Shaul, David L.

1981 Semantic Change in Shoshone-Comanche, 1800–1900. *Anthropological Linguistics* 23:344–355.

1986 Linguistic Adaptation and the Great Basin. *American Antiquity* 51:415–416.

Shimkin, Demitri B.

1980 Comanche-Shoshone Words of Acculturation. *Journal of the Steward Anthropological Society* 11:195–247.

Smith, Ralph A.

1959 The Comanche Invasion of Mexico in the Fall of 1845. *West Texas Historical Association Year Book* 35:3–28.

1960   Mexican and Anglo-Saxon Traffic in Scalps, Slaves, and Livestock, 1835–1841. *West Texas Historical Association Year Book* 36:98–115.

1961   The Comanche Bridge between Oklahoma and Mexico, 1843–1844. *Chronicles of Oklahoma* 39:54–69.

1963   The Mamelukes of West Texas and Mexico. *West Texas Historical Association Year Book* 39:65–88.

1970   The Comanche Sun over Mexico. *West Texas Historical Association Year Book* 46:25–62.

1973   Bounty Power against the West Texas Indians. *West Texas Historical Association Year Book* 49:40–58.

Sowell, Andrew Jackson

1884   *Rangers and Pioneers of Texas*. San Antonio: Shepard Brothers and Company.

Tate, Michael L.

1971   Frontier Defense on the Comanche Ranges of Northwest Texas, 1846–1860. *Great Plains Journal* 11:41–56.

Thomas, Alfred B.

1929   An Eighteenth-Century Comanche Document. *American Anthropologist* 31:289–298.

1941   *Teodoro de Croix and the Northern Frontier of New Spain, 1776–1783*. Norman: University of Oklahoma Press.

Thurman, Melburn D.

1988   On the Identity of the Chariticas. *Plains Anthropologist* 33:159–170.

Turpin, Solveig A.

1982   *Seminole Canyon: The Art and Archaeology*. Texas Archeology Survey Research Report 83. Austin: University of Texas.

1989   The End of the Trail: An 1870s Plains Combat Autobiography in Southwest Texas. *Plains Anthropologist* 34:105–110.

Viscaya Canales, Isidro

1968   *La invasión de los Indios bárbaros al Noreste de México en los años de 1840 y 1841*. Materiales para la Etnohistoria del Noreste de México 2. Monterrey: Publicaciones del Instituto Tecnológico y de Estudios Superiores de Monterrey.

Wallace, Ernest, and E. Adamson Hoebel

   1952   *The Comanches: Lords of the South Plains*. Norman: University of Oklahoma Press.

Wistrand-Robinson, Lila, and James Armagost

   1990   *Comanche Dictionary and Grammar*. Norman, Oklahoma: Summer Institute of Linguistics.